Finance Unleashed

Magnus Lind • Kelly Barner

Finance Unleashed

Leveraging the CFO for Innovation

Linda—
BE the lion!
KKBarner

palgrave
macmillan

Magnus Lind
Skanor Group Ltd
London, United Kingdom

Kelly Barner
Buyers Meeting Point
Shrewsbury, Massachusetts, USA

ISBN 978-3-319-66369-2   ISBN 978-3-319-66370-8   (eBook)
DOI 10.1007/978-3-319-66370-8

Library of Congress Control Number: 2017954400

Cover illustration: © Tom Brakefield / Getty Images

Printed on acid-free paper

This Palgrave Macmillan imprint is published by Springer Nature
The registered company is Springer International Publishing AG
The registered company address is: Gewerbestrasse 11, 6330 Cham, Switzerland

Praise for *Finance Unleashed*

"I have been Innovation Director as well as CFO, and currently I have both responsibilities. I firmly believe the CFO should be a major driving force for innovation, in strategic decision making, portfolio management, budgeting, working capital management, restructuring and so on. This book captures these subjects; I recommend everybody to embrace the ideas in it!"
—Paul Smits, Innovation Director and CFO, Port of Rotterdam Authority

"The financial supply chain is real, and this book presents it as a cohesive element rather than a string of disconnected links. *Finance Unleashed* provides a practical model to illustrate how successful companies can navigate the coming transition. This book will forever change how you regard finance and the role of the CFO."
—Robert Davis, Former CFO of CA, Inc.

"Lind and Barner present how nonfinancial companies can lead change through financial disruption and how it can dramatically increase competitiveness, profitability and customer acquisition and retention. They place the CFO at the center of this transformation and captivate the reader by describing what financial disruption means for the CFO, CEO, and the Board. It is an inspiring must-read."
—Lena Apler, co-founder and Chairman at Collector Bank, and fintech investor

"*Finance Unleashed* reinvents the CFO's office and puts it into the center of strategic business leadership. I'd recommend it to anyone looking for a model for how successful non-financial companies can deal with coming changes."
—Christian Lanng, co-founder and CEO, Tradeshift

"Magnus and Kelly have captured essential insights into the often over-looked but complementary roles of finance and procurement. In today's risky environment, the need for these two corporate partners to align strategies to bolster enterprise value and build resilient supply chains is more important than ever. Insights into the tradeoffs between price competitiveness, working capital, the total cost of ownership, and visibility into financial and operational analytics are all captured in practical insights in *Finance Unleashed*. Financial and supply chain analysts alike should read this book and start working together to create health supply chain balance sheets and longevity of relationships for the future."

—Robert Handfield, PhD, Bank of America University Distinguished Professor of Supply Chain Management at North Carolina State University, and Executive Director of the Supply Chain Resource Cooperative

"The collective innovation capacity of our supply partners vastly exceeds that of any one organization on its own. But what role can the CFO play in unlocking this enormous source of competitive advantage? *Finance Unleashed* provides both the inspiration and a practical model for Finance executives to deliver revenue growth and reduce internal costs by facilitating supplier-led innovation."

—Philip Ideson, Managing Director of Palambridge and Founder of the Art of Procurement

"Lind and Barner wonderfully bring together the key facets and implications of the 'mash up' of the financial and physical supply chains driven by the De-globalization and Disintermediation of the Banks and the emergence of digitalised manufacturing supply chains. The positioning of the book, fre-quently written from a CFO perspective operating on either side of the finan-cial institution or manufacturing and supply chain fence, really helps to translate global economic theory into the key aspects and challenges of future corporate strategy."

—Nick Ford, Executive Director, Odesma

"Lind and Barner take the wraps off an undiscovered opportunity: When guardians of finance use the power of cashflow to unleash innovation in their suppliers, the result is increased value for suppliers, buyers and the buyers' customers. This is an innovative and important premise and one that CFOs need to act on. *Finance Unleashed* shows how."

—Donal Daly, Executive Chairman, Altify

"*Finance Unleashed* is a pledge to finally address issues that have been hindering business relationships for too long. Both Procurement and Finance need to evolve from a tactical role to an enabling one. As the testimonies and interviews of a very diverse panel of experts illustrate, there are many opportunities and reasons to close the disconnect between the physical and the financial supply chain (and between Procurement and Finance). The book is a call to action to focus less on operational technicalities and more on the meaning of business."

—Bertrand Maltaverne, Senior Business Consultant,
JAGGAER, Procurement Digitalist

"Digital transformation has affected so many areas of modern business (technology, communications, data, and intelligence) and yet it has left the financial supply chain largely untouched. Lind and Barner point out that elevating intelligence and streamlining corporate processes—especially those that affect the supply chain—are the keys to value creation, innovation, and sustained competitive advantage."

—Stephany Lapierre, CEO, tealbook

"Digital disruption and new trading behaviours require a paradigm shift in the financial and supply chain world. This book clearly focus on this dilemma and eminent need for upscaling the financial- and supply chain system in todays 'modern society.' *Finance Unleashed* shows that companies can grasp new opportunities in the world of end-to-end supply chain management, however it requires a fundamental shift in the use of financial instruments and a significant adoption of the business models and governance structures. The authors can be complimented for a book with a very pragmatic approach."

—Kees van der Vleuten, former Chief Procurement
Officer of Fokker Technologies and Tennet TSO

"This book is a must-read for anyone in finance looking to increase corporate competitiveness and to add new sources of customer value. The *Finance Unleashed* model also pushes for the importance on making finance cheaper, faster and more optimal. It is paramount that the political sector gains this knowledge in order to ensure growth and wealth in a time where technology changes the financial landscape fast. Don't miss it!"

—Lars Arne Christensen, Chairman of the board at Infiniance,
Board member in Copenhagen FinTech, Candidate for the Danish
Parliament for the Conservative Party

Are you frightened by the lion?
Or,
Are you the lion?

Foreword

Innovation has – and always will be – the holy grail for creating value for an organization's customers and shareholders. While this drive is nothing new, the pressure is now on to accelerate the process of innovation. The result is market-leading companies looking outside their organization's walls for assistance and inspiration to increase the speed, flexibility, and resilience of their supply chains.

Suppliers – once 'merely' the source of goods and services required to fuel a company's operation – have become a fertile, trusted source of creativity, collaboration, and competitive advantage. I have been studying outsourcing and strategic sourcing for years, monitoring the changing nature of relationships between companies and their product and service suppliers. The lessons are clear; today's business models – including an organization's contracting, performance metrics, and payment processes – must be re-examined to take into consideration the paradigm shift needed to support an ecosystem of collaborative business partners.

Sadly, the financial supply chain does not work as smoothly or transparently as we might expect in the 21st century. Far too often the very suppliers we look to for innovation and risk mitigation are being cash-starved by the way their customers handle payments and working capital. Many companies are making the all-too-common mistake of thinking about the physical (goods and services) and financial (cash) supply chains as intersecting at the point of payment. Unfortunately, this limited view ignores the fact that just as the physical supply chain is a progression from raw materials to finished goods, the financial supply chain is a long series of transactions running in constant parallel to the physical chain. Today's supply chains demand digital transactions be completed smoothly and quickly if leadership teams are to possess the capital required to fund innovation. To be successful, today's CFO and supply chain professionals must shed old habits and conventions that are preventing their financial supply chain from making its full contribution to competitive advantage.

Finance Unleashed takes a fresh look at an age-old problem: how can businesses accelerate the pace of innovation in a time of global trade and fragmented supply chains? This book sheds new light on this challenge by bringing together first-hand perspectives from executives and thought leaders, providing the reader with an engaging exposure to a broad range of business approaches and management styles. I believe the importance of this book will only increase in the long term as organizations continue to seek ways to ease the friction between their physical and financial supply chains.

Although this book is targeted at the finance and the CFO communities, there are pearls of wisdom in it for leaders in all functions: procurement, supply chain, business development, and treasury, not to mention the CEO. Magnus and Kelly artfully point out that a 'whole chain' perspective on innovation requires internal alignment and the very best that each functional area can bring to the table.

High praise is due to Magnus and Kelly for bringing the topic of financial supply chains to the forefront of the business world. I look forward to seeing how the global business community responds to the ideas and philosophy behind *Finance Unleashed*.

Faculty – Graduate and Executive Education,   Kate Vitasek
University of Tennessee Author, educator,
and architect of the Vested business model

Preface

According to Toyota,[1] it takes just 18 hours to manufacture a customized car. And yet, even as of 2016, it could still take as long as 48 hours to process a cross-border payment for the car – an accounting transaction that never requires the funds to exist in a distinct physical form. Considering that each payment consists of no more than a few debit and credit transactions, there is a huge opportunity at hand for anyone willing to invest resources into improving the flow – and the transparency – of the financial supply chain (FSC).

In addition to this unnecessary inefficiency, the prevailing overemphasis on working capital as a preferred financial performance metric creates systemic problems. Large companies inadvertently force their suppliers – including companies a mere fraction of their size – to 'finance' their operations by stretching payment terms as long as possible. This not only places a disproportionate cash flow burden on small companies, but also stifles innovation by withholding funds from the very organizations in the supply chain best positioned to use it for the creation of broad and sustained value.

Although transaction speed and cash flow concerns are pressing, they are both symptoms of a larger problem: the tactical nature of most finance organizations. Today's competitive markets demand that everyone in the organization, from the warehouse floor to the executive suite, maintain a customer-centric perspective in the execution of their work. The only way finance can earn the distinction of being truly (rather than nominally) strategic is to tie every decision they make to the value created for the company's end customer.

Today's rapid rate of innovation has created a series of paradoxical disconnects between the speed of business and the speed of finance. The unnecessary complexity and delay in the FSC are where the opportunity lies for those prepared to seize it. This is therefore a broad strategic issue, naturally affecting the CFO, but including the CEO and the board.

Illuminating interactions, such as those that happen during roundtables and executive conversations, have repeatedly proven to us the value of hearing unique and authentic perspectives on the FSC from diverse groups of leading professionals. This led to the interview-driven approach we have taken in this book. *Finance Unleashed* was written to inspire you by sharing the vision and perspective of select corporate and public sector leaders on the FSC conundrum – in their own words. We have intentionally kept it direct and concise so you can be energized and fueled by many new ideas in a short time.

Based around a series of interactive interviews with global influencers and executives, this book challenges readers to think laterally and to find inspiration in new ideas based on their experiences and research. Some of the voices represented here are those of old friends and colleagues and others were connections deliberately made in order to have their distinct perspective represented in this book.

We see the evolution of the FSC as the natural next step for global business. Our aim is to present the financial supply chain from a strategic rather than a tactical or operational perspective. We aspired to create a book to serve as a catalyst for leaders who are in a position to make meaningful changes today. Fast moving and to the point, this book is for people of vision and action and for anyone who is sincere about creating good conditions for growth, innovation, and increased employment.

Skanör, Sweden   Magnus Lind
Boston, MA, USA   Kelly Barner
July 2017

Note

1. "How Long Does it Actually Take to Make a Car?," Toyota.co.jp, Accessed January 14, 2017, https://www.toyota.co.jp/en/kids/faq/b/01/06/.

Acknowledgements

*To all the Small and Medium Sized Businesses
who struggle to get paid on time.*

*To all corporate executives searching for increased competitiveness,
and to all of the up-and-coming professionals eager to join their ranks.*

Our purpose in writing this book is to convey the unique opportunities financial disruption provides for non-financial companies. We want to inspire and keep the discussion on a strategic level rather than on an operational/tactical level. We decided early on that the book should be fast to read and intuitive, and introduce different perspectives and ideas from practitioners – in their own words. The book is intended for forward-thinking corporate executives who want to solve the constant conundrum of how to remain competitive (or even increase competitiveness) so his or her company can be successful.

We want to thank our interviewees for kindly spending their scarce discretionary time sharing their valuable insights and knowledge with us so we can share them with you. Their contributions provided us with the diversity of perspective required to better understand and illustrate how the financial system works and how future trends are likely to affect our ways of working.

We are deeply grateful to Susanna Bondéus for finding and introducing us to our interviewees. Susanna also triggered our decision to go ahead and write this book and supported us along the way. Without her, this book would not have happened.

It has been very rewarding for us to speak and discuss with all our interviewees. We especially want to thank Peter Huber for spending so much time and effort to develop a model using the process view on the financial supply chain. It was during a lunch in Malmö, Sweden, while preparing for the agenda of The Talent Show conference in April 2016, that Magnus and Peter got the idea to define the financial supply chain as a full process in its own right rather than it just being regarded as a supporting process. We now draw it in parallel to the physical supply chain, from the customer to the suppliers. This opened up new models for how to approach rationalization and introduce Lean Six Sigma.

Since our first meeting in 2010 with Sir Charlie Bean, then the deputy governor of the Bank of England, he has been very supportive of the corporate perspective. Magnus met Charlie the first time with a large number of corporate treasurers to discuss the effects of the new financial regulation and the disintermediation of banks vis-à-vis corporates. They have had many meetings since and Charlie has a natural gift for structuring and communicating his vast knowledge and experience of how the financial system works. Charlie has been very important to us for much more than this book.

Tim de Knegt, Murat Erden and David Loseby have been instrumental and very supportive in developing the model presented in this book. Their thought leadership and 'can-do' spirit come across clearly in their interviews where they present forward-looking visions and ideas that can serve as inspiration for all of us.

Dr Adrian Atkinson's model of wealth creators is a breakthrough for understanding the differentiation of leaders who do exceptionally well and those who do great. This is based on his vast academic and professional experience and unique research with senior executives spanning over two decades. We are glad and grateful to have been able to document his research and model here, one that is highly relevant to the new, emerging role of the innovative CFO.

Murat Erden represents executives who have innovated with a customer perspective, something we place firmly at the center of the transformation of the corporate financial supply chain. We are glad he accepted our invitation to present his accomplishments in this book.

We also thank the communications team at Turkcell for the care and effort they invested to help us share their story with detail and accuracy.

Thanks to Gary Slawther, Jack Miles, and Luis Manuel Hernández for presenting their different views, methods, and viewpoints on the role and challenges and tools of the CFO as well as the other organizational functions he or she must work with side by side.

Without Kate Vitasek, who has long been an amazing example, mentor, and friend, this book would not have come to print. There are no words to express our gratitude for the support she provides without desiring anything more in return than that we push ourselves to achieve our full potential.

Given that at the time of writing Kelly has three children, aged 9, 7, and 4, her husband Craig deserves many thanks (and a beer) for being supportive and understanding of the effort and sacrifices required to write a world-class book from the kitchen table.

We also wish to thank David Desharnais for sharing his vision of the future of the financial supply chain and adding many essential parts and pieces of the thoughts behind this book. We reference his holistic view of the supply chain and we have used his expression – the "ecosystem play" – throughout the book.

Magnus and Kelly also want to extend their gratitude to Gerard Chick for putting them together in the summer of 2016, when they clicked on the idea of writing a book by bringing the perspectives of purchasing and finance together in one place.

Finally, we reach out to Rebecca Lind for helping the appearance of our figures match the clarity and style of the vision, and Alexandra Lind for all her support and care. We also (sort of) express our gratitude to the 'iGeneration' of Johan and Oscar Bondéus for eyeballing (modern: 'iballing') Magnus whenever he asked them 'dinosaur' questions.

Skanör, Sweden
Boston, MA

Magnus Lind
Kelly Barner

Contents

List of Figures

Part I

Background

"*The world is changing very fast. Big will not beat small anymore. It will be the fast beating the slow.*"
– Rupert Murdoch

1

Three Critical Changes to the Role of CFO

Magnus Lind and Kelly Barner

The role of Chief Financial Officer (CFO) has historically been an internally focused one. Even when their sphere of influence and interaction did stretch beyond the four walls of the corporation, finance's top priority remained supporting the needs and objectives of their own organization. In some cases, this led to finance being pushed to meet and exceed performance targets at the expense of suppliers and distributors: the very partners they were dependent upon for innovation and competitive advantage.

The notion of a well-managed 'Financial Supply Chain' (FSC) has been around for decades, and the topic has received increasing attention in recent years. But what exactly does it mean? It is fine for onlookers to have a general sense of the FSC, but for those in positions of execution or leadership, the burden of understanding is (and should be) much greater.

Being able to make the distinction between Supply Chain Finance (SCF), which centers around financing techniques, and the FSC, which tracks the movement of capital, risk, credit, and cash through the full series of financial transactions in the supply (and demand) chain, is essential. Looking at such broad activities requires us to take a holistic view of the supply chain instead of focusing on a singular enterprise's balance sheet.

M. Lind
Skanor Group Ltd, London, UK

K. Barner
Buyers Meeting Point, Shrewsbury, MA, USA

© The Author(s) 2018
M. Lind, K. Barner, *Finance Unleashed*, DOI 10.1007/978-3-319-66370-8_1

From our perspective, here is the meaning of each phrase:

The <u>Financial Supply Chain</u> (FSC) is the movement of capital, cash, risk, and credit back and forth between parties in the supply chain. The FSC extends from raw material producers, through multiple processors, to points of sale, and finally to the end consumer. Although there are differences between the number and types of parties involved, Business to Business (B2B), Business to Consumer (B2C), and Business to Government (B2G) commercial arrangements all have Financial Supply Chains.

<u>Supply Chain Finance</u> (SCF) is a financial program put in place by a company that makes lines of credit available to their suppliers in an effort to simultaneously increase supplier access to affordable funding and decrease their costs. The capital for an SCF program may come from the purchasing company's working capital or be arranged as a line of credit through the company's bank on behalf of their suppliers.

When we use the phrase 'supply chain' we mean the full supply and demand chain, incorporating the whole flow from the first supplier to the end-consumer.

The unanswered questions for companies new to working with the entire financial supply chain are nearly endless:

- How do all the available IT and financing solutions relate to each other? Are they different or the same?
- How do the solutions fit into the larger corporate context and is pushing Days-Payable-Outstanding (DPO) the correct metric for today's corporations?
- What if the money we release through SCF is spent and our credit rating drops, making it hard to continue funding the program?
- How can we achieve transparency through the whole supply and demand chain rather than stopping with first tier suppliers and distributors?

Everyone willing to explore the FSC is a visionary in their own way. These influencers are putting important changes in motion simply by establishing a discourse with their peers, an open and challenging discussion about the FSC: what it is and what it can become. This mindset represents a new approach to finance that has the potential to become an extremely powerful force reaching far beyond its own remits.

If SCF is *supplier-centric*, then the FSC is *customer-centric*.

Finance does not work in isolation. The FSC is an 'ecosystem play', both internally in the company and in conjunction with external stakeholders. Legacy finance practices are focused on reporting and compliance, making the CFO manage a disparate group of departments, often with diverging objectives and even different 'languages'. The CFO has often had a singular balance sheet view and cannot continue in this mode if they are to increase the scale of their impact.

In response to the rise of customer-centric finance as a corporate goal, we formulate the following three concepts, which it is critical for the CFOs of today and tomorrow to understand and embrace:

1. *Finance must take a customer-centric view* if they are to be firmly grounded in the core business of the enterprise. All activities in finance should be evaluated for the benefit they create for the end-consumer, a practice which effectively erases the silos created through diverging priorities and focus.
2. *Take a process flow perspective* so that finance is not relegated to being an intermediary or supporting function operating and optimized as a silo. Instead, the flow of capital and risk from the first supplier to the final end-customer can be optimized using Lean Six Sigma-type methods to streamline the financial supply chain.
3. *Allow the whole supply chain to innovate.* This is most likely to happen if we ensure that capital, available credit, and risk are distributed optimally over the whole financial supply chain. Chains that leverage the capabilities of the whole ecosystem significantly decrease the long-term risk of corporate survival.

We cannot caution strongly enough against the limitations resulting from a finance organization that is focused on a single internal purpose. Even once we have expanded our perspective so that it appropriately includes the other internal and external stakeholders in the financial supply chain, the next step will be to place an emphasis on the correct activities and priorities and streamline our objectives and strategies.

Being customer-centric doesn't always come naturally for CFOs, treasurers, CPOs, or the head of accounting. Instead, these professionals have been trained and incentivized to focus on a two-dimensional spreadsheet version of the operation rather than the full three-dimensional effort itself. They risk becoming isolated as kings or queens in their own kingdom, one that falls increasingly out of alignment with the business as a whole. This is a recipe for building silos, and the longer it is allowed, the thicker the walls become. It might seem far-fetched to make accounting articulate the value they create for customers on a daily basis, and yet we believe with the right mindset this is entirely possible.

One way to break a siloed perspective is by regarding the movement of capital, risk, and credit as an uninterrupted flow so we can apply proven techniques from Lean Six Sigma to enforce customer-centricity and sort out what creates value and what does not. Transforming finance from a 'supporting' process to a 'core' process is instrumental to making the role of finance strategic.

Customer-centricity repositions single balance sheet strategies such as extending payment terms to allow for the reduction of working capital by pushing it up or down the supply chain. The consequences of pushing payment terms out to the detriment of suppliers, something we refer to as the 'working capital dogma', is common as a practice and as a performance metric for finance. It can create unnecessary risks by reducing the amount of capital available to suppliers to invest in innovation. Innovation is inherently risky and requires cash. With less available cash, the risk of failure increases and the delivery of successful innovation decreases. Pushing working capital out into the supply chain effectively outsources capital investments to suppliers. Conversely, taking capital out of the supply chain by extending payment terms 'insources' responsibility for innovation to your own company, perhaps even without the assistance of supply partners. That might not be such a clever thing to do.

2

Finance Taking a Customer-Centric View

Magnus Lind and Kelly Barner

The ultimate goal of any company is to sustainably increase the level of stakeholder value they create. As a result, the primary stakeholders are their customers, since they are the key source of financial value and long-term commercial survival.

Fostering the conditions under which full customer value can be created is no small task. This leads many experts and influencers in the business world to label value-oriented efforts as 'strategic'. Unfortunately, this term is often applied as a form of wishful thinking rather than an accurate designation. The word 'strategic' has become both overused and misused. The appeal of its implied importance often obscures the need to set apart certain tasks as being higher level or more intellectual than others.

Things that are important aren't necessarily strategic.

Merriam-Webster defines the term strategic as "of or relating to a general plan that is created to achieve a goal in war, politics, etc., usually over a long period of time."[1] If we follow this definition to where it intersects with the focus of this book, strategic activities are those that benefit the customer and therefore generate sustainable financial gains for the enterprise. Those gains must then be converted into the potential for future growth, regardless of

M. Lind
Skanor Group Ltd, London, UK

K. Barner
Buyers Meeting Point, Shrewsbury, MA, USA

© The Author(s) 2018
M. Lind, K. Barner, *Finance Unleashed*, DOI 10.1007/978-3-319-66370-8_2

whether that potential originates from within the company's own walls or from the way they interact with the rest of the supply chain.

When finance enables the generation of expanded, sustainable revenue streams, they are strategically relevant. Process improvements, real-time reporting, and making the operation more cost efficient may be complex, necessary, innovative, and even revolutionary, yet these efforts are only tactical unless they also create discernible value for the customer.

Finance with an Entrepreneurial Hunger

When finance is a strategic resource, it places an almost singular focus on customer retention and acquisition. It is no more complicated than that. Consider start-ups as an example. Most start-ups are 'bootstrapped', meaning that they are founded without the backing of venture capital. These lean companies realize very early on that a focus on customer value – understanding what their customers care about and finding a way to satisfy their demand profitably – is a must. Venture-backed companies often don't need to have quite as complete an understanding of their customers. At least initially, they only need to satisfy the wants and needs of their backers and investors.

This may be the reason for the underperformance of so many venture capital (VC)-backed companies. There are estimates that only 1 or 2 in 10 – or a maximum of 20% – of VC-driven enterprises deliver significant returns. As a 2012 *Wall Street Journal* article explained, "The common rule of thumb is that of 10 start-ups, only three or four fail completely. Another three or four return the original investment, and one or two produce substantial returns."[2] Even venture capital-backed start-ups need to place their customers at the heart of their efforts sooner or later. To convert customer focus into a successful business requires sharp attention to value creation and raw ambition and grit. This approach must be part of the company's DNA from the boardroom to the operating floor.

To achieve top to bottom alignment on customer value creation, expectations must be very clear. Here are the two things Chief Executive Officers (CEOs) and board directors of large corporations have told us is important for their finance team to embrace:

1. Knowing your field is just the base of the CEOs' and board's expectations.

   Few board directors know the details associated with each part of the business (treasury, finance, supply chain, procurement, etc.) simply because it isn't necessary. Instead, the board expects each function to satisfactorily perform their operational and tactical tasks as a baseline. In order to be perceived as a high achiever and outperform against expectations, finance has to keep the customer in mind (i.e., become strategic) and deliver to the top and the bottom lines in the short, medium, and long term. Every function must contribute to the core business of the company. This requires a team of corporate generalists with expert level knowledge in their field that they are able to apply with lateral thinking.

2. Do not dwell on outcomes and history; walk forward boldly into the future.

The board is much more interested in what is yet to come because they can no longer influence the past. Work alongside management and focus on how you can contribute an increasing level of value going forward. How can finance provide value to the end-customer? Employ a forward-thinking attitude and a broad commercial mindset at all times.

These seem like straightforward points, but inevitably the inconvenient reality sets in. How can you do this practically? How will you find the time? You have so many reports to deliver, so many decisions to make, so many systems to implement, and so many meetings to attend. It is important to consider the possibility that your current situation is a direct result of how you have worked in the past. Ask yourself whether you are trying to achieve a *future* result with a *legacy* approach. Find a new way to meet base executive expectations, such as by automating or delegating reporting and data management, so that you can exceed those expectations by putting the customer at the center of all financial efforts.

Your Best Strategy Is to Make Yourself Redundant

In some cases, requests for additional resources will be purposely ignored or dismissed, perhaps because the board needs you to refocus and deliver more with less. You must make hard choices: streamline, automate, outsource. Identify your most important deliverables – not from a functional perspective, but from the point of view of the customer. Prioritize the list and estimate the percentage of your time that you will dedicate to each deliverable. Anything that does not make the list is not worth your energy. This kind of approach may create stress, yet it is difficult to find the will to stay sharp or to innovate in a comfortable environment.

If stress is bothering you, change your attitude toward friction. Instead of rejecting the pressure it causes and allowing it to make you feel uneasy, regard it as your personal trainer. When you want to improve your physical performance, you work with a personal trainer because he or she will force you to deliver more, to train harder, and, ultimately, to succeed. Stress can function as an intellectual trainer: always present and sometimes yelling. Embracing stress will enable you to invoke your survival instincts and achieve what needs to be done to transcend adversity and stagnation.

Your current workload is a direct result of how you organize your tasks and team: both the intentional and the unintentional consequences. Instead of setting out to be a delivery machine, focus on what you can do each day to make your work more efficient and contribute strategically to the business. Study how to incorporate business modeling. Read industry reports. Get to know your company's customer-facing teams so you can ask them about their pain points to understand how you can relieve them. Meet with your company's customers (and even their customers) to understand their wants and needs. Engage with entrepreneurs and adopt their rationale and thinking. Look for ways to increase conversion rates in the shop, via your website, or wherever you meet your customers. Decrease your customers' friction to buy.

In the words of Steve Jobs:

> When you grow up you tend to get told that the world is the way it is and your life is just to live your life inside the world. Try not to bash into the walls too much. Try to have a nice family life, have fun, save a little money. That's a very limited life. Life can be much broader once you discover one simple fact: Everything around you that you call life was made up by people that were no smarter than you. And you can change it, you can influence it... Once you learn that, you'll never be the same again.[3]

Too often, individual decision-makers put the corporate equivalent of 'walls' in the way of their own progress. We regard policies, processes, and frameworks as fixed when they are really just organizational habits instilled over time. The more habitual a task, the less likely it will create value for the customer. This often puts us in the position of targeting the very tasks and habits we find most familiar as the first to eliminate when we make the move to become more strategic.

If a role is deemed to be tactical because it does not add value for customers, isolate it, and make that position redundant. Many things are important without being strategic. Strategy increases customer acquisition and retention; period. To add value you must think like a bootstrapped start-up or an entrepreneurial CEO whether you are in finance, treasury, procurement, or elsewhere.

How Can Finance Provide Customer Value?

International travelers have a perfect opportunity to witness first hand an example of how finance can improve both revenue and profit generation. At the airport, once you have made your way through security, travelers pass by duty-free shops that are designed to optimize the shopping experience for someone who: (a) has limited time; and (b) is on the move. You pass stands for alcohol, perfume, chocolate, and other well-displayed luxury items. It is easily accessible and there is always someone to help you find what you are looking for. The shopping is fast, enjoyable, and convenient, until…

Until it is time to pay for the goods you have selected. Then you are forced into a long line decorated with boring shelves offering candy, cheap deodorant, and other small convenience items. The payment experience can take up to 75 percent of the total shopping timeline. At this point, many customers are lost because the payment friction is too high.

The cash registers (finance) represent an unintentional impediment to closing the deal with willing customers. Too often, especially when the friction is limited to the payment or cash flow portion of the exchange, companies seem to accept that there is no alternative but to suffer through the inefficiency and wait for the transaction to process regardless of how long it takes. Where the responsibility for improving this situation lies is often unclear. As a result, IT, the Chief Financial Officer (CFO), and the treasurer all too often distance themselves from the role of being the customer facilitator. When that happens, these teams can take the opportunity to create customer value or shy away from it because they do not view it as part of their 'core' responsibilities despite its strategic importance.

What is the use of developing an attractive store offering if the payment process determines whether the customer buys or not? This is a perfect example of how finance can either create strategic value or become a roadblock to customer value and top- and bottom-line growth.

Continuing with the previous example, we do not believe that finance sets out to make the commercial process inconvenient – any more than the duty-free shop says, 'Let's make the payment process a difficult as possible.' They simply might not be thinking about the experience from the perspective of the customer. This is an opportunity for finance to dramatically scale the value they create – viewing the entire purchase and payment process from the customer's perspective.

Welcoming 'Disruptive Finance'

We believe that the time is now right to invest in finance-led innovation that significantly – as opposed to incrementally – changes the dynamics of a company or industry. This could include offering cheap and easily accessible customer financing to lower the threshold for selling a product such as the UPS/DHL case study provided in Chapter 11. 'Disruptive' means that your competitors are affected negatively and the way of doing business in your industry is changed profoundly.

There are two alternatives to disruptive finance. One involves 'incremental' improvements such as providing cheaper financing for suppliers. This provides opportunities to lower prices, but it is not so dramatic that it significantly affects customer behavior or forces the competition to respond with a strategy of their own. The effects of incremental change are primarily contained within the walls of the company, and they are imperceptible to customers, suppliers, and the competition.

The other alternative to disruptive finance is to change nothing at all. As disappointing as incremental change might seem, this is far worse. The world is changing at a rapid pace, rendering traditional practices obsolete practically overnight. Leaders and decision-makers who choose to do nothing are either in denial about the rate of change or abdicate their responsibility in the face of it, preferring to view themselves as victims of an 'unstable' system rather than fortunate opportunists in the midst of circumstances ripe for action.

Global competition is fierce and only the strong will survive. In our opinion, the key to that survival is creating and maintaining customer value. Financial disruption has provided finance with the ability to create incremental customer value by reducing payment friction (for example), and, if finance is strong and visionary enough to push further, it is within the reach of the CFO to disrupt an entire industry.

Notes

1. "Strategic," *Merriam Webster*, Accessed July 6, 2016, http://www.merriam-webster.com/dictionary/strategic.
2. Deborah Gage, "The Venture Capital Secret: 3 Out of 4 Start-Ups Fail," *The Wall Street Journal*, September 20, 2012, http://www.wsj.com/articles/SB1000 0872396390443720204578004980476429190.
3. Art Digital, "Don't live a limited life, (Steve Jobs motivates you in less than two minutes)," *YouTube* Video, 1:06, September 25, 2015, https://www.youtube.com/watch?v=WilF7TVIgXI.

3

Take a Process Flow Perspective

Magnus Lind and Kelly Barner

According to Toyota, it takes 18 hours to manufacture a customized car.[1] And yet, even in 2016, it still could take 48 hours to process a cross-border payment. Considering that each payment consists of no more than debit and credit transactions, the 30-hour difference between these physical and financial chains demonstrates just how much we can gain by investing resources into improving the flow – and the transparency – of the financial supply chain.

Finance is currently regarded as a support to the core business. Support areas and their processes can only have a limited impact on the corporation because they are contained within one or more silos. When finance adopts a customer-centric methodology that includes the full ecosystem of suppliers and distributors, it is possible to transform finance from a supporting process into a core business process. When finance is successful, the financial supply chain will have the opportunity to become the center of innovation and dramatically support the changing role of the Chief Financial Officer (CFO).

Finance is not the only function with processes that need to be broadened. System-wide process improvements in the physical supply chain have proven very successful in delivering improved customer value. With just-in-time, Lean Six Sigma, and all their cousins, we have developed methodologies for prioritizing, structuring, and implementing meaningful lasting improvements. The basis for all these improvements is being able to regard the physical

M. Lind
Skanor Group Ltd, London, UK

K. Barner
Buyers Meeting Point, Shrewsbury, MA, USA

© The Author(s) 2018
M. Lind, K. Barner, *Finance Unleashed*, DOI 10.1007/978-3-319-66370-8_3

Production Time

48 hours?!   ## 18 hours

Cross-Border
Payment

Fig. 3.1 It takes 18 hours to manufacture a car and up to 48 hours to send the cross-border payment for the car (as of 2016). Which chain offers the greatest potential for efficiency gains: the physical or the financial chain?

supply chain as a seamless process with minimal stationary inventory on hand and a constant reduction of waste and inefficiencies. The key is getting the flow of the process, in which finance can be transformed from a series of supporting processes into one core, seamless process that extends beyond company borders. Improvements in the physical supply chain are consistently driven on an overall level. By managing 'the flow' of the FSC, it can be managed on an overall level as well.

This transformation of the financial supply chain is primarily centered around the CFO and his or her distinct office. In the past, process improvements and customer acquisition and retention were predominantly connected to the process flows associated with goods and services. The CFO was hired to make sense of it all; to report and comply while the CEO and other functional leaders innovate, sell, and develop.

Since the disruptive center of gravity has moved to finance, the CFO is now squarely in the middle of change rather than watching and supporting it from the sidelines. Few CFOs signed up for a role that requires such strong general business acumen. In order to deliver the desired improvements, CFOs need to lead the shift to a primarily customer-driven focus, one that makes the financial organization an active innovation center. And yet, this is not all. Besides innovating, the CFO is still expected to report and comply just as before. It is a very challenging – and at the same time rewarding – time to work in finance.

Finance's legacy as the guardian of reports, compliance, and governance has split the function into siloed sub-organizations with limited cross-pollination. Even when enterprise-wide transformational efforts spill over into finance, the focus isn't on process improvements or innovation. For instance, Lean Six Sigma in finance often centers around financial data rather than customer data. The siloed approach not only serves as a roadblock to improvement, but

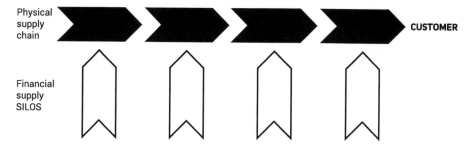

Fig. 3.2 The physical supply chain (in *full black*) is usually depicted as a flow while the financial supply chain (framed white *block arrows*) is chopped up into siloed 'supporting processes'. This doesn't support a supply chain view and may lead to a suboptimal distribution of financial resources and unnecessary costs and time delays

it has also led to finance becoming a 'cobbled-together' organization, containing everything from accounting and procurement to IT and treasury.

When we talk about the 'finance process' we are referring to the process of transferring money, risk and credit from an account through booking, payments, or other financial transactions involving the complete supply chain. Although we can describe the finance process as holistically as physical flows of goods, it is far more disjointed and is usually managed as series of discrete steps. This is where we must start to rethink the finance function – in the mapping and rolling out of it as a cohesive and fluid process.

For several years, we have heard that the banking sector is being disrupted by new technology, especially from fintech (an abbreviation of 'financial technology'). This is certainly the case, but it is unlikely that the financial processes in non-financial corporations will remain unaffected by fintech disruptions in the financial system, including improved methods for payments, risk management, and lending and investing. It might even be the fact that the financial process offers much larger opportunities for improvement to non-financial industries, in terms of both waste reduction and also releasing the capital tied up in inventory and extended payment terms forcibly 'offered' to suppliers.

What if you could transparently view the flow of cash from the customer (order to cash) all the way to the supplier (purchase to pay) as one long process, continuing to do so in the whole chain in other companies in your ecosystem, in the same way as in your own? What if we applied the same methodologies for improvement to the financial supply chain as we do to the physical chain? What would you be able to achieve as an organization? How would you be able to structure and approach the financial process? What metrics could you use to measure and track performance or contributions to operational health? If you continued up and down the chain, extending the effort outside your own company remits, what benefits could each participant in the chain realize? How

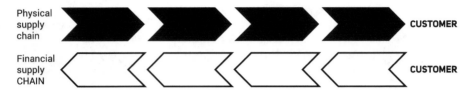

Fig. 3.3 The financial supply chain represented as a consistent flow, within each company and between all companies in the supply chain. This perspective changes how finance can holistically leverage available opportunities, reduce costs and time delays and allocate financial resources more optimally

could the whole chain benefit? What could your customers' benefits be? Could it improve your competitiveness?

In fact, many of the functions that report into the CFO's office often have difficulty understanding each other. They don't share a 'common language', which obviously raises barriers. The procurement department (which often reports to the CFO) doesn't always regard themselves as financially driven. The introduction of Supply Chain Finance (SCF) has served as an example of how two functions reporting to the CFO can be made to work together; treasury and procurement. SCF is a solution that requires a cross-functional support and implementation effort. Treasury is measured on working capital and procurement is measured on total cost. In fact, by introducing SCF, fintech vendors and banks have done non-financial corporations a huge favor by showing the way that cross-functional finance development can happen.

The next level of sophistication requires the whole finance process to be mapped out from the supplier to the end-customer. With a core process flow view, the CFO can attack the whole process using proven methodologies and techniques.[2] The next step is to mimic the dynamics of the physical chain, including both demand and supply chain parties in joint improvement and innovation efforts.

Notes

1. Toyota Children's Question Room, *Toyota*, accessed February 27, 2017, https://www.toyota.co.jp/en/kids/faq/b/01/06/.
2. For information on making this approach a reality, consult Chapters 8 and 15 for perspectives on behavioral procurement and Lean Six Sigma-influenced financial metrics, respectively.

4

Allow the Whole Supply Chain to Innovate

Magnus Lind and Kelly Barner

Small and medium-sized businesses (SMBs) need financial assistance from other organizations in the market. This is not a result of the way they manage their operations as much as it is a function of the leverage disparity between them and their much larger customers. SMBs would need less of other organization's money if they were allowed to have increased access to their own. Instead, they are forced to 'invest' in their customers through extended payment terms, even when those same customers have a significantly stronger cash position than they do.

The global GDP is valued at roughly US$120 trillion and the average estimated payment turnaround is 60 days. This can translate into as much as US$20 trillion in outstanding or unpaid invoices globally on any given day. Add to this the fact that nearly US$2 trillion is paid in transactional payment fees every year[1] and large ongoing investments strand a huge amount of capital in payment float at any given time.

Policy makers have tried to solve this problem by printing money, a decision that inadvertently encourages SMBs to increase their debt – thereby layering on additional costs and risks. Why should this have to be the case when most SMBs have enough money in the first place? In practice, regulations effectively prohibit bank funding for SMBs, meaning that newly printed money does not end up with them anyway. Sadly, most government policy efforts to regulate and add excessive liquidity to the markets have created a circular error.

M. Lind
Skanor Group Ltd, London, UK

K. Barner
Buyers Meeting Point, Shrewsbury, MA, USA

© The Author(s) 2018
M. Lind, K. Barner, *Finance Unleashed*, DOI 10.1007/978-3-319-66370-8_4

With the rapid and continuous development of the physical supply chain, finance executives have oceans of inspiration and case examples to explore when looking to improve the financial supply chain. One particular area of focus is cross-company cooperation to distribute capital and risk in the supply chain. A survey of senior purchasing executives conducted by The Boston Consulting Group and the Procurement Leaders Network in early 2013 provides us with this inspiring quote:

> In 1989, when Chrysler was fighting for its life, its president of operations, Bob Lutz, and its vice president of procurement, Tom Stallkamp, brought in 25 of the company's biggest suppliers and asked for their help in reducing costs. "All I want is your brainpower, not your margins," Lutz told the suppliers. Buyer-supplier collaboration caught on at Chrysler, thanks to the company's willingness to share the benefits, and in the ensuing decade, the program[2] (called SCORE, for Supplier Cost Reduction Effort) produced billions in savings.[3]

The Chrysler strategy is also relevant for the financial supply chain, and provides evidence of how finance executives can engage suppliers and distributors (and maybe even customers) to channel their collective experience and knowledge for innovation and financial process efficiencies. In this light, working capital projects that outsource work processes such as vendor data management seem old-fashioned. In fact, the above quote from 1989 seems more contemporary than ever.

Executives at large corporations may sit around and consider what it means to be good corporate citizens, but if they accept deliveries and then wait months before paying for them, their efforts are misplaced. Narrow-minded working capital targets place a company's own balance sheet at the center of what matters. In today's complex web of physical supply and demand chains, we must also take an ecosystem view of the financial chain. The siloed approach that so often creates operational problems has a negative impact on a company's approach to finance, preventing them from taking advantage of process-driven or cross-functional opportunities. Besides funding, this applies to the management of foreign exchange and commodity risk volatility.

In 2016, American Express conducted a study about SMB business planning an effort to shed light on the role that the financial ecosystem plays in fostering innovation.[4] In a survey of 250 CFOs from Australian companies with revenues of between $2 million and $300 million, AmEx concluded, *inter alia*, that SMBs don't invest sufficiently in innovation in large part because of a lack of available cash. This, in turn, forces the large companies in the chain to shoulder a disproportionately large role in product development and innovation.

The best way to expand innovation capabilities is by exploiting the intellectual capacity of the whole chain at once as Chrysler did. The challenge is that almost every large, publicly listed company has working capital targets that incentivize them to push debt up and down the supply chain – in other words, anywhere but in their own accounts.

Consider these recommendations regarding the best use of a supply chain's combined liquidity and what effect it can have on supply chain innovation and competitiveness.

Large Companies with Cash Holdings Can Release SMB Funds

Instead of accepting negative or relatively low interest rates for less productive investments, large companies can help their SMB stakeholders avoid having to borrow at 20 percent or 30 percent. Lack of SMB liquidity presents a serious risk for corporations of all sizes. As Chris Dark, the president International for C2FO, a global fintech company, wrote for *Supply & Demand Chain Magazine in 2015,*

> Economies are currently suffering from a paradoxical situation of having too much liquidity in certain areas while having too little in others. Banks, awash with cash, are reluctant to accept deposits; larger corporations are stockpiling cash but running out of options of where to place it; while small to medium-sized businesses (SMBs) are often unable to access funding. Many SMBs are facing a liquidity crisis as a result, which is a direct risk to corporations' supply chains.[5]

As he rightly points out, liquidity itself is seldom a problem because central banks make cash abundant; it is the distribution of cash in the economy that is a problem – particularly for the SMBs.

Large Companies Can Partner with SMBs to Avoid Being 'Unbundled' by a Myriad of Start-Ups

In April of 2016, CB Insights wrote about the challenge consumer packaged goods (CPG) conglomerates such as P&G are facing from the smaller players in their many market segments. "…With a portfolio of brands spanning skin care, hair care, cleaning goods, pet food and more, P&G is now under attack by a host of companies looking to inflict a 'death by a thousand cuts' on the

$220B giant."[6] Mobilizing an ecosystem of SMBs could be a good defense strategy for these large companies. Historically, their strengths were based upon having a huge sales force and dominant brands. These components lose some of their power when start-ups can use much cheaper means to reach the same customers and build an independent brand ultra-fast with considerably fewer investments.

Large Companies Can Leverage the Naturally Strong Linkage Between Innovation and Survival in an SMB

The owners and executive management team at an SMB usually suffer much more personally in the event of the company failing. This risk functions as a powerful incentive to innovate. Since innovation must come from within, being core to the company's DNA, it must also be a primary executive priority.

Taking a full ecosystem view that includes the whole supply and demand chain makes it possible (and worthwhile) for SMB stakeholders of large companies to partner with them to protect and even foster future market growth. Large companies could give SMBs their own money back instead of forcing them to act as banks – simply by paying them closer to the actual delivery and when the goods change ownership. This re-establishes the opportunity for them to innovate with the support of liquidity that many times actually belongs to them.

The relative importance of working capital targets and innovative competitiveness look very different when seen through a financial ecosystem point of view – as do the true costs of the working capital dogma.

Notes

1. Marc Niederkorn, Phil Bruno, Florent Istace, et al., "Global Payments 2016: Strong Fundamentals Despite Uncertain Times," *McKinsey & Co.*, September 2016, http://www.mckinsey.com/gsa/clientlink/global-payments-2016-strong-fundamentals-despite-uncertain-times.
2. John Braun, Mark Guthrie, Emily McCampbell, and Violetta Sit, "Chrysler Corporation: Innovations in Supply Chain Management", *University of Michigan Business School*, accessed February 28, 2017, http://www-personal.umich.edu/~afuah/cases/case3.html.
3. Robert Tevelson, Jonathan Zygelman, Paul Farrell, et al., "Buyer-Supplier Collaboration: A Roadmap for Success," *bcg.perspectives*, August 21, 2013, https://www.bcgperspectives.com/content/articles/sourcing_procurement_supply_chain_management_buyer_supplier_collaboration_roadmap_for_success/.

4. "Opportunity for innovation highlighted by 2016 American Express CFO Future-Proofing Survey," *PASA Procurement,* June 2, 2016, http://procurementandsupply.com/2016/06/opportunity-innovation-highlighted-2016-american-express-cfo-future-proofing-survey/.
5. Chris Dark, "The Liquidity Paradox – A Risk to Your Supply Chain," *Supply & Demand Chain Executive Magazine*, March 30, 2015, http://www.sdcexec.com/blog/12059795/effectively-mitigating-this-risk-is-critical-to-secure-existing-operations-and-enable-growth-ambitions.
6. "Disrupting Procter & Gamble: Private Companies Unbundling P&G and the Consumer Packaged Goods Industry," *CB Insights Blog*, April 19, 2016, https://www.cbinsights.com/blog/disrupting-procter-gamble-cpg-startups/.

5

The CFO as the Driver of New Business

Magnus Lind and Kelly Barner

The role of the CFO is changing, and CEOs have a part to play in deciding just how much change will be ushered in through the head of their finance function. If the CFO is to drive new business and innovation, appointing the right CFO is one of the most strategic decisions a CEO can make.

Every big change must start from the top, and so the burden of setting a good example rests with the CEO. Any CEO who is focused on driving high and sustainable growth by improving customer acquisition and retention should consider the opportunities presented by financial disruption. It is surely too good an opportunity to pass up.

It is now possible to eradicate economic waste in the form of unnecessarily tied-up capital, high interest charges and fees, and wasted lead times, as well as to create opportunities to provide stickier, stronger, and more extensive offerings to current and prospective customers. An open-minded CEO can create completely new markets and demand for new and current offerings with the support of a like-minded CFO. The opportunities do not end in each company's 'local' part of the chain; they are available throughout the entire supply chain.

Given this opportunity, how can CEOs kick-start organizational change through finance?

The first step is to evaluate whether the current organization and management team measure up, paying particular attention to the CFO. The financial

M. Lind
Skanor Group Ltd, London, UK

K. Barner
Buyers Meeting Point, Shrewsbury, MA, USA

© The Author(s) 2018
M. Lind, K. Barner, *Finance Unleashed*, DOI 10.1007/978-3-319-66370-8_5

disruption we see today has forced CFOs into the center of new business opportunities which may require a journey through unfamiliar territory.

When a new company is founded, the leadership team usually starts to consider hiring a CFO once the complexity created by customer- and product-facing units (such as sales and manufacturing) need someone to ensure that it abides by statutory reporting and compliance. This 'command and control' part of the CFO role centers around the company's own income statement and balance sheet, which remain in the CFO's remit. In addition to this, a customer-centric CFO is also an innovator – someone with a strong general business acumen. For many CFOs, this new expectation requires them to make career-altering adjustments to their perspective and objectives. Harder still, it may not be what they signed up for, or in the realm of what they aspire to do.

As was noted earlier, every big change must start from the top. If significant changes are to be made in the finance organization, the CFO has to serve as a good example for finance, just as the CEO has to serve as a good example for the corporation as a whole. The qualities of each CFO are more important than ever because today the CFO's role is more challenging and strategic. When command and control are combined with innovation (especially disruptive innovation) and lean financial production methods, it makes the CFO remit almost as lateral as that of the CEO.

Does your CFO measure up or does he or she aim to maintain the current 'command and control' role as long as possible? CEOs need to face a tough fact: in order to affect the kind of change they desire, the CFO should be CEO material. Whether they are in line to take over the role in the current company or at another, the potential should be there for them to excel in a customer-centric financial organization.

Consider the financial supply chain as a process that runs parallel to the physical chain. The financial chain is the flow of money in the direction opposite the flow of goods and services. Taking this point of view will help you see the financial chain as far more than a support process. You can use current tools and methodologies, introduce incremental improvements, and reduce economic waste. There have already been many successful attempts to apply Lean Six Sigma to the financial supply chain, as Luis Manuel Hernández describes in Chapter 15.

Be careful where you focus your efforts, as many organizations have attempted to use a solely data-driven view as the centerpiece to implementing financial Lean Six Sigma methodologies. We believe the CFO should enforce a customer-centric view, as defined and discussed in Chapters 2 and 10. Ensure that the entire organization maintains a customer-driven perspective by designing performance metrics that can measure it. Although metrics are important, they should never be so prescriptive as to stifle innovation. Metrics can measure the results of innovation, at least in traditional categories of value, but they can not inspire or directly create it. For more on this, read about the important art of how to inspire (rather than dictate) innovation touched upon by Murat Erden in Chapter 7.

Some financial teams have already taken a leading role in fueling top-line growth. In Chapter 11, we describe how UPS and DHL have added financial services to their customer offering. Now they not only pick up and deliver their customers' physical goods, but also finance them, making their offering stickier, more attractive, and more competitive. In our contacts with corporate executives we see increasingly that, as in the case with UPS and DHL, the financial chain is merging with the physical chain.

Companies that own the relationship with their customers, and provide them with a valuable product or service, are frequently adding financial components to their offerings as a way of becoming indispensable. The banks and fintech providers, as illustrated in our UPS and DHL example, take roles as suppliers to UPS and DHL, who often retain ownership of the end-customer relationship.

Finally, CEOs should expect the CFO to be excited enough to embrace the financial supply chain as the most strategic opportunity for growing the customer base and advancing the company's competitiveness. CFOs that simply agree with the CEO about the need for change will not – indeed, cannot – lead to the same corporate impact as CFOs who are actively engaged in the process of driving change. The role of 'command and control' must operate flawlessly as it has in the past, but under this new model it becomes a secondary priority. Some CFOs might struggle with the need to move beyond this traditional role.

Since the CFO's office is a mixture of disparate functions, including controlling, accounting, IT, procurement, and treasury, it may contain different subcultures and even different 'languages' as presented in Appendix 1. The functional divide in the CFO's office is usually archaic. Examples of cross-functional cooperation are few and far between. This is slowly changing, though, and we have seen positive examples over the last few years, such as treasury and procurement finding common ground through supply chain finance programs, allowing them to serve as a catalyst for new value. Lack of cross-functional cooperation is nothing new. We had a similar situation when just-in-time and *kanban* approaches were first being implemented in the physical chain, some 40 years ago. They too had functional barriers to overcome.

The CFO should consider appointing one person as responsible for financial supply chain integration to enforce this cross-functional mindset and serve as the single point of contact, internally and externally. There are many vendors of financial supply chain solutions struggling to find this single person to assist companies to leverage their modern technology and solutions. The single point of contact is a crucial and senior appointment requiring lateral experience and the ability to cover and understand how innovation and supply chain management work.

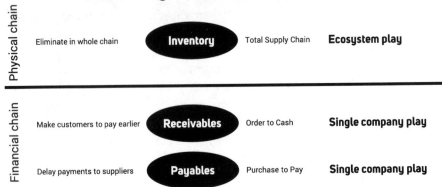

Fig. 5.1 There is a remarkable difference in how we perform working capital projects as a single company play rather than in an ecosystem play as we usually do in the physical supply chain. The idea for this picture came from a handbook in working capital management

Don't 'navel gaze' your own balance sheet. Steer away from the single company working capital dogma described in Fig. 5.1, which presents the different approaches between physical and financial supply chains, an ecosystem play versus the single company plan. That no longer works.

The CEO and CFO must work jointly to face the challenge of convincing investors and the corporate board of the need to change to a modern, broad, working capital mindset. Such a change may lead to more vertical integration in supply chains, catering to increased quality, fostering and investing in innovation and new techniques, and reducing financial costs and risks. Tesla, with the unconventional and innovative CEO Elon Musk at the helm, seems to have taken this strategy to heart.[1] The company is a proponent of vertical integration when they need to solve issues such as capital distribution and innovation capabilities and control. Outsourcing up and down the supply chain does wonders for balance sheets, while creating vulnerabilities in the current disruptive environment where intermediaries are circumvented. Is Tesla also disrupting this legacy of capital distribution? Is vertical integration a strategy to evaluate? Do your working capital targets allow you to evaluate vertical integration as a strategic option?

Elon Musk does not allow short-term metrics stop him from innovating, breaking legacy approaches, or pursuing a long-term purpose and goal. The truly disturbing fact about the working capital dogma is that it restricts the number of strategies an 'addicted' company is able to choose between. That can also put the company's long-term survival at stake. The strategy should be long-term while many accounting metrics are short-term. The strategy should rule the metrics, not the other way around.

We believe that even if CEOs are hesitant to introduce vertical integration, they should still consider taking a full supply and demand chain view. This is especially true if the company is the biggest player in the chain. They must involve all relevant stakeholders in the work of implementing the 'lean' management of money. In Chapter 8, David Loseby presents the benefits of using a behavioral model for the supply chain while driving financial benefits, which can be used as a 'soft' way to vertical integration without acquisitions and mergers.

When just-in-time and *kanban* methodologies were first implemented some 40 years ago, the objective was to decrease and eventually deplete safety inventory between machines and then, later, between suppliers. If we regard unnecessary capital as just a form of safety stock, we can identify and reduce pockets of tied-up capital instead of just pushing it up and down the chain. There are massive inefficiencies and opportunities to explore in current trade finance practices as described by Gary Slawther in Chapter 13.

When you consider the supply chain as a holistic entity designed to serve customers, you have a very different vantage point than what current financiers see when they evaluate each link of the chain separately for credit. A 'link' view also reduces the opportunities for technical integration and transparency. Why, for instance, do we have so many payment transactions in one single chain if there is only one end-customer? Taking a full supply and demand chain view alters the picture dramatically when transacting financially, and it provides a glimpse of what opportunities lay in modernizing the financial supply chain. Tim de Knegt addresses these points in Chapter 6.

Pretend for a moment that we are back in the 1980s or 1990s, managing the physical supply chain. We would force cross-functional cooperation and increase focus on customer value, gradually streamlining all processes. Over time, we managed to break down resistance to change, developed a shared language, and reduced contradicting metrics. We expect the methods we used at this time (and which have improved since) to work as well in the financial supply chain as they do in the physical chain.

CEOs and CFOs could consider engaging in benchmarking groups to help their company develop in line with its peers. Generally, non-financial companies have lagged financial companies in their adjustment to new financial technology and processes. There is generally no lack of technology, as Tim de Knegt discusses in Chapter 6, but there *is* a lack of adoption. By focusing on the big picture and being able to comprehend the whole supply chain – including all stakeholders – new opportunities to create customer value are discovered. And for the largest company in each chain, the juiciest improvements are likely to be found outside of their own balance sheet.

Without financial value no other value can be created.
Customers are the source of long-term financial value.
Therefore, only the activities that increase the customer base and perceived customer value can be considered strategic.

Note

1. Fred Lambert, "Tesla is now ~80% vertically integrated, says Goldman Sachs after a Tesla Factory visit," *Electrek*, February 26, 2016, https://electrek.co/2016/02/26/tesla-vertically-integrated/.

Part II

Perspectives

"The biggest problem is not to let people accept new ideas, but to let them forget the old ones."
– John Maynard Keynes

6

Visions for the Financial Supply Chain

Tim de Knegt

Summary

Our capacity for real, meaningful change is limited in part by our imagination and in part by the true desire to change. Although it is easy to point fingers, technology generally serves as more of a conduit than a barrier. In fact, revolutionary technology usually exists long before individuals and organizations are willing to take advantage of it. As a result of human hesitancy, the more that can be centralized – whether through technology or controls – the easier and faster it becomes to carry out the change that is at hand.

Interview with Tim de Knegt conducted September 28, 2016

My background as corporate treasurer, head of strategic finance, and as a lateral business person has given me a clear vision for the innovation and development of the financial supply chain. Innovation represents much more than just technological innovation, which is part of the total cycle that people and companies go through. Innovation is anything that propels us forward, improves a current process, service, or product or adds a new process, service, or product. In my opinion, there are three types of innovation to move us forward: *technological* innovation, *social* innovation, and *legislative* innovation. This is my vision for the financial supply chain.

Real innovation tends to flourish when there is a direct need or when existence is threatened. Usually this is led by military innovation. Examples

T. de Knegt
Head of Strategic Finance & Treasury, Port of Rotterdam Authority,
Rotterdam, Netherlands

M. Lind, K. Barner, *Finance Unleashed*, DOI 10.1007/978-3-319-66370-8_6

include the developments of nuclear weapons in the 1940s, the Space Race during the 1900s, and the development of cars in the early 1900s when cities' sanitary systems were threatened by horse manure.

The threat of financial warfare and the innovation taking place in other sectors threaten the existence of the financial sector in its current form, making further development of the financial supply chain imminent.

Legislative innovation often drives what governments can do when it comes to promoting innovation, but if the change is not allowed, or if we don't know how to regulate it, then there is no way to move forward. When we don't fully comprehend how we can use something or if there is no perceived benefit, we tend to move away from it. A good example of legal innovation in the financial supply chain is how governments deal with unregulated systems such as Bitcoin. Legal innovation in many cases also relates to social innovation created when we embrace the use of a product, system, or process.

One of the major technical innovation trends is digitalization (or the so-called "Internet of Things") where data will be interconnected. Everything will be connected to the Internet and everybody will be connected to one another. We have seen significant connectivity growth in the last couple of years and this is expected to continue towards 50 billion devices connected in 2020. However, this is still only 2.7 percent of all devices. The Internet of Things includes robotics, virtual reality, and artificial intelligence. Digitalization is the major proponent for the growth prospects we have globally.

The other trend is the energy transition. We're moving away from petrochemical products toward clean energy. If we combine the two latter trends, we can see that there are two major revolutions happening at the same time. As it so happens, the financial supply chain is caught in the middle of them.

Growth Through Digitalization

There are two ways to grow economies or businesses. One is by reducing costs and the other is by adding products and services. Digitalization supports both. When you look at the energy transition, cleantech replaces the petrochemical-based system, a trend toward growth that is also bolstered by digitalization. The cleantech transition will transfer power and wealth from one group of companies and people to others. We can therefore add social innovation to the list of changes taking place.

We have already seen that, for instance, when Tesla acquired SolarCity, they advanced their transition from storing energy in a battery in someone's house to using cars as mobile batteries that can move from point A to point B due to the production of energy through the solar panels. The combined solar panel, battery, and car are not just production and storage devices, but also a translation device for the energy.

When you look at the financial supply chain, you see this innovation in energy together with the Internet of Things. In fact, when you take a supply chain perspective, there are many points connecting both of these innovations.

Right now, the complete financial supply chain is intermediate. There are limited interfaces, and there is no one, holistic approach to the financial supply chain like we see in the logistical (physical) chain. If Nike purchases shoes or purchases the goods to make shoes, they must know every company within the entire supply chain because they have to ensure that there is no child labor (for example) and that everything remains compliant and functions smoothly. This is partly due to the disintermediation caused by jurisdictions and legal entities.

If the holistic approach is already increasingly implemented in the logistical chain, why doesn't it also happen in the financial chain? I think it will happen in the near future. Since all the data are already connected, the logistical chain will continue to be optimized; even delays of a few minutes matter. This means that the much simpler (because it's only data) financial chain must also improve because the two chains can't have too large of a productivity deviance.

The rapid evolution of logistics, where we improve the tracking and tracing of everything, must serve as the blueprint for the evolution of the financial chain, including the knowledge of where the margins and pricing concerns are. And with all the information that we have access to, crowd prediction and automated decision making can help improve it further. All of this will feed into the physical chain and eventually spill over into the financial supply chain.

The financial chain is currently in a kind of transformation. A good way to describe it is to compare it to the revolution from the wooden ships we saw in the sixteenth and seventeenth centuries to the warships and 24,000 TEU container ships now sailing the oceans. I believe today's financial supply chain is still one of those wooden ships from the sixteenth century. The difference is that we won't have to wait as long for the financial transformation to be complete.

This will be an intense transformation. Systems will be more decentralized as we see a move away from asset-based business models. The same will be true for the financial supply chain. The money will be made, not necessarily by the person holding the cash, but by whoever can interpret the cash or the data in such a way that they can give viable information to whoever needs it. Those who can operate their business model with less financial resources will have increased their advantage over the competition.

We are likely to see something like what is taking place in the energy sector. There is a mediation between infrastructure companies who make limited revenues, whilst the returns go to those that give the right advice or provide the products (v. the infrastructure). Going forward, money will be part of the 'infrastructure' v. part of the service, given how much money is available as a result of monetary easing. Cash is on its way to becoming a commodity and soon it won't be able to generate the kind of returns that we saw a decade ago.

System-Wide Shift in Business Models

With the expansion of the Internet of Things and Big Data we also see a shift in business models. It is no longer necessary to just sell your product (for instance, a car) on an incidental basis, because you can also sell it through a service (priced per kilometer driven) with additional services (traffic, maps, etc.) that can be offered to the whole industry and not just your own brand of car. These products and services will also need to be paid for through the financial supply chain and the current system is not able to accommodate the explosion of transactions which will be caused by the billions of devices which will be connected to the internet in the next decade or so.

And this brings us to the question: What will help us generate the necessary returns in the future when the value of money stabilizes? What will be so valuable to us that it will be the main form of value exchange? It is a crucial question to answer as it could also mean a redistribution of wealth.

Traditional financial principles are the base on which banks make credit decisions from analyzing each link in the supply chain. They don't necessarily look at the complete supply chain as one single, combined entity. My view on this is when people talk about supply chains, they often see only the individual nuts and bolts linking parties together. They focus on one-to-one relationships, and when you have a lot of one-to-one relationships loosely tied together we call it a supply chain. In my view, the future supply chain will consist of many-to-many relationships; you will have the relationship between yourself, your counterparty, and your counterparty's counterparty, ad infinitum.

We reap the benefits when we centralize data from all our counterparties and feed all our counterparties the information relevant to them. In essence, it's like Twitter where everybody interacts with everybody and nobody is excluded from the conversation. Open data is a very important concept when it comes to many of these relationships because that is the only way we can help each other.

Assume you do business with a particular counterparty with whom you have a good relationship but they cause pain to another party in the supply chain. Maybe your relationship is affected even though the pain is not caused by you directly. This instills governance or social policing, because the chain as a whole will still determine how each link treats the others.

The data are something that we should share with the whole group of companies and individuals that are trying to work together to provide consumers and/or businesses with a service or product. Competition should be instilled on the speed of development, drive for innovation, and growth as well as competencies in terms of analytics. Data is the commodity that should be available to all, and information is what differentiates competition.

When it comes to the importance of whole chain transparency, I have some ideas on the solutions that are being developed to increase that transparency. Take the PacMed example, for instance, a medical solution for general practitioners (GP) where the GP adds the patient's symptoms. PacMed analyzes millions of patient data points looking at other patients' reactions to treatments and medication to find those most aligned and suggests treatments and medications. There is no sharing of personal data. This is a very good example of where privacy concerns can be addressed while the data is still used for the betterment of others. Anonymization of data will be a very important feature when enabling transparency.

Another relevant example for the financial supply chain is the development around supply chain visibility. Large components of total supply chain costs, and thus our products, are in fact caused by inefficiencies and perceived risks. If we are able to reduce the unknown steps in the chain by means of transparency, we will realize a significant reduction in total supply chain costs, and, more importantly, will improve the trust between companies and individuals. Lastly, I firmly believe compliance with rules and regulations can be captured by this method as well, ensuring further developments in the legal innovation that is necessary for economic development.

If you look at what makes companies and nations successful, the key capability is how well they adapt to change. That is what made the USA great in the 1940s, 50s and 60s. That is what made Europe great. That is what made Japan great during the '80s, and Southeast Asia in the '90s. That is one of the biggest challenges you see right now; Western countries are not keen to change. Increasing transparency will make it clear that they need to change without actually serving as a catalyst. The same conditions apply to lagging companies; the best-known examples are Kodak, who went down due to a lack of change, and Apple, who reinvented itself on the brink of bankruptcy to become the company we know today.

Transparency and distribution of information create the need for adaptable, distributed systems. Centralized systems are too slow to adapt and will therefore be threatened. We are likely to see a big social disruption where central powers are challenged by faster and nimbler distributed systems.

I believe there is no single solution because there is no single best way forward. Though I believe that something needs to change, this can only be accomplished together with other like-minded companies and individuals. We are probably moving toward a system where everybody's voice counts and can even bring about changes in our democratic system. That is where the Internet and energy revolutions can take us. Taking us to a system of distributed information to ensure distribution of wealth to ensure everyone benefits, a system where the different forms of capital (Material or Manufactured, Financial, Social, Intellectual or Human and Natural Capital) are all represented.

Moving Away from Centralized Systems

We have been talking about three models: a centralized system, a decentralized system, and a distributed system. We've always seen that we start with a decentralized system which later turns into a centralized system. It happens at all levels: governments, energy systems, company structures, etc. Now we are seeing a move away from centralized systems. In certain countries, it is more prominent than others. If you look at Africa or India, for instance, little is centralized yet and therefore they can move faster towards a distributed system, which is a many-to-many system. In fact, Africa is extremely competitive in financial disruption being first with real-time payments. An example of this is M-Pesa, the African real-time payment and microfinancing service. M-Pesa allows users to deposit, withdraw, transfer money and pay for goods and services easily with a common mobile device.

The challenge for developed nations is that their systems are centralized, and as we move toward a distributed system we have no clue what the implications will be.

We have a system where a vendor provides a product to its customer and gets paid 30, 60, or 90 days later. What are the prospects of reducing the payment slack? My view is that the current payment terms are part of the problem, or at least a component of it. A much bigger problem is the number of payments that happen in one supply chain. For example, take a container ship moving from China to Germany and going through 20 different kinds of companies creating 20 legal transfers of ownership and 20 payments. Why do we need 20 different transactions for one logistic delivery, and why do we need this to inflate the cost of production for the end-user? We have already taken out slack in other industries where this was the case in the past, for example travel agents and the taxi industry. We will see disruptions in logistics soon as well.

On the one hand, you have the payment terms which make it very difficult to achieve transparency. Where the payment terms do make sense is in a retail environment where if you buy the products from the distributor and it takes you 60 days to sell it in order to get the money to pay your distributor, but then payment terms are part of the supply chain conversion from business to business to business to consumer.

However, if you can take all of the risks out of the system, and what I mean by that is that if you know for sure that you will sell your products within 60 days, then there is no reason for the financing to be at any different cost than the cost of the payment terms. Right now, the cost of the payment terms is not necessarily separated within the transactions because once you buy a product from a distributor it is just part of the operational expense of the product. Whereas if you rent or if you borrow the money, it becomes part of your financial income and expense and that hits a different part of the profit and loss statement.

Many companies seem not to realize that by reducing their payment terms they can actually reduce operational costs and make their business more viable by making the cost of the payment term more transparent. Working capital management is already an important part of the business model, but could be further integrated. It is very important to connect the payment terms with the logistics, ultimately leading to a lot more transparency around the actual cost of each part or service.

Since transparency is a key element, reducing payment terms would help bring about more transparency, and a reduction of volatility, into the financial system. It would also reduce the need for derivatives and hedging products, currently a major challenge for central banks.

I would not agree we are lagging in technical innovation since the technical solution is rarely a problem. The problem is that the users of the system and the owners of the data within the system don't work together. A technical solution is already there most of the time, even all the data is there. It's just a matter of mapping it together and bringing it all to the surface. Innovation will not happen until the social innovation happens because people want to work together and the government creates the environment in which these products and/or services can flourish.

Natural Limits of Connectivity

If you're trying to create social innovation within an existing group of 50 or 60 people at the same time, it can be hard. If you're able to do it with one or two, and then those two can be the frontrunners telling everybody what the benefits are and why it's so important to be part of this social innovation, then the two will become three, four, five, etc. It's often easier to start small with a minimal viable product rather than going out to 50 people at a time.

That's also why I don't believe in examples where there are 40 or 50 banks already involved in the same system. For instance, R3, a consortium of circa 70 large financial institutions, is putting in the effort to create an open-source Blockchain platform called Corda. When you have 50 parties involved in the system trying to innovate through consensus, there is a risk that all they will do is talk. They try to convince each other that the road they're taking is the right one while they're not actually going anywhere.

I am involved in several Blockchain initiatives, being distributed systems by design. Where and how and when will they be implemented? The Blockchain name is quite new, it started with just a few members back in 2008. However, it is very similar to the concept of relational databases that has been around since the 1980s. In essence, Blockchain is a relational database. With the upcoming Internet of Things and everything connecting to the Internet, the concept of relational databases has changed. Much more data is available and much more information needs to be transmitted back and forth to allow for a common understanding on what happens where and for what reason.

I don't think that the question is whether the data-sharing concept that Blockchain promises will make it or not. I think the question is to what extent and when will Blockchain make it in combination with other concepts like virtual reality and artificial intelligence, and to what extent will it redefine the economy and financial system as we know them today?

One good example is a concept around social housing called "Blandlord". It's built on Blockchain and turns rental houses into small companies. They divide each house into small shares, and as a personal investor it is possible to invest in a house on a specific street. The value of the house increases or decreases like a share price, and the rental income that you get from the house is like the dividend. There are many other applications of this concept.

Whatever needs to happen in the move from the petrochemical-based system to a clean-based system is another example of where you can use Blockchain. This is also true for new circular electric systems and circular economies.

Another example is a system where chips are built into firearms so that the GPS signals where a gun is fired. If that happens, it will send a message to the police and it will track where the gun was fired. The person that fires the gun is connected to a biometric system so only he or she can fire the gun.

It sounds a bit like George Orwell's *1984*, yet I think the combination of all this data can only be viable or interesting in the context of a Blockchain/relational database environment. This combination redefines how we value trust and transparency.

Conclusion

Tim de Knegt puts the financial disruption into a societal context and lifts it above accounting, reporting, procurement, and treasury. He is the kind of finance leader who focuses on the company as a whole first.

While Tim doesn't directly address customer requirements, he does discuss the fact that finance represents their organization, identifies the need for ongoing changes, and owns technical solutions that create new value for people in general. He goes beyond customer-centric and takes a human-centric perspective.

Tim is very specific when he discusses how new technology improves transparency in process flows and enables new forms of interaction that enhance cooperation and business model development. These will eventually change the concept of trust, how we value each other, and how we choose who to cooperate with. Building on the process flow concept, Tim describes his expectation that the static chain will be replaced in communities where bigger, stronger parties are being overtaken by those that are faster and nimbler. If the distributed model takes root, it will transform the centralized models we currently work within.

Key Take-Aways

- Humans, not technology, are the true barriers to meaningful change. Many of the innovations coming to market today require not only process or structural changes, but also alterations in human perspectives.
- Some changes, such as improvements to smartphones and other consumer electronics, take place gradually in response to user demand and feedback. Other changes, such as the shifts Tim observes in the financial supply chain and energy sector, are based on foundational systemic shifts that take place beyond the sight of most people.
- There are three types of innovation: technological, social, and legislative.
- Right now the financial supply chain is intermediate; it is not as seamlessly connected as we often see in the physical supply chain.
- Although the transformation of the financial supply chain may be overdue, change will come much faster than we have historically seen with similar kinds of change.
- The determination of what holds the greatest value (i.e. currency vs. data) will also dictate who is in power at any given time.
- Technology is often available (or at least possible) long before humans are prepared to leverage it. The ability to adapt will therefore play a significant role in determining who becomes the market leader going forward.

- We can observe the transformation from centralized to distributed systems in the public sector, energy sector, company structures, etc. This will likely have huge ramifications on democracy, distribution of wealth, compliance, and business models.

Tim de Knegt is a well-rounded finance professional with a track record of defining and implementing effective strategies, engaging teams, and delivering transformational change. He is currently responsible for the strategic finance and treasury activities at the Port of Rotterdam Group, which includes the following functions: group treasury, business control, investment management and governance of subsidiaries. He is also a promoter of the game-changing innovation community at the Port of Rotterdam, which stimulates internal as well as external innovation.

7

The Innovator CFO

Murat Erden

Summary

All organizations and executives will agree that innovation is important for sustaining competitive advantage, and yet, when it comes to making that innovation a reality, remarkably few succeed. If meaningful – and potentially disruptive – change is to become a reality, innovation must be distinctly assigned and given support at the highest levels of the company. Of course, even purposeful investment in innovation does not ensure success. Companies that are serious about systematic innovation must be willing to accept, and in some cases even celebrate, the periodic failures that will inevitably play a part in motivating change. Here Murat paints his picture of how the CFO role is changing and the importance of innovation in finance.

Interview with Murat Erden conducted August 11, 2016

I have found that the finance function is becoming more strategic and that the shift is affecting finance professionals. Going forward, I believe finance will increasingly focus on how they can make a significant difference to the company. If you look at performance numbers all around the world, the low productivity of many companies is evidence of the problem. It is easiest to observe when you analyze companies that have been at the top of their markets (often globally recognized names and listed/traded companies). Many of them have moved to a lower ranking or are diminished from their former

M. Erden
ice group, London, UK

© The Author(s) 2018
M. Lind, K. Barner, *Finance Unleashed*, DOI 10.1007/978-3-319-66370-8_7

stature because they couldn't find the right way to continue at a high enough level of productivity to keep their markets engaged going forward.

It used to take a company 50 years to go from 'loom to doom'. Now we see corporate life spans decreasing to 15 or 20 years. It seems quite likely that over the course of the coming decade we will see many of the firms which are currently listed as the highest market cap in their space replaced by companies we have not yet heard of. This 'turnover' is happening much faster because of available technology and the convergence of products and services. With this background, I believe many shareholders and corporate executive teams are spending too much of their time on day-to-day jobs while completely missing bigger picture strategic issues. Therefore, it is necessary to have a dedicated strategic role in each executive team, whether it is the CFO, the CEO, the CTO, or someone else.

You can argue that we are organizing our companies in the wrong way. Each team is optimized to handle one discrete function. That type of arrangement tires and wears us out and then we are expected to use weekends, off-site retreats, occasional meetings in the corridor, and board meetings to become strategic for a while. I don't believe there is anything wrong with our standing format, but it is necessary for companies to adapt to our new and fast-changing world. How should the members of the board and the executive team prepare to meet these changes? Almost everyone has already understood this need, but often there is little to no change in the way leadership is conducted and no organizational development plan to take us from here to there.

I believe the critical issue is that we need to have sufficient awareness. We know the world is changing fast and we need to adapt, but we don't devise clear plans for responsibility and ownership. Innovation often remains a shared responsibility, one that is a secondary task only addressed after the tasks associated with the functional role are completed. Who is responsible for helping the company adapt to a constantly changing environment? I believe I have only rarely seen that there is one person responsible for this. Often the transition focuses on short-term actions related to the annual plan. I believe innovation is a transition that requires a much longer-term perspective.

Should there be a dedicated person responsible for innovation in the company? Should that person be strategically placed to be able to influence others and maybe even have a dedicated team? If that is the case, and you only have one senior person responsible, isn't there a risk that all the others capitulate and say, well, if he or she is responsible, then we don't have to work on innovation? They might actually cement the old way of working functionally. That is definitely a risk, so let's challenge ourselves with a situation where there is no one specific person responsible versus a situation where there is one person responsible for innovation. It is, after all, not a black and white issue.

When the executive team is bogged down by short-term objectives and targets, they accommodate innovation briefly during annual meetings or at off-site retreats where they spend a few days naming incentives. 24 hours after the event, no one gives innovation any thought until one week before the next meeting – yet another condensed retreat where the circle continues with no real progress having been made.

If we instead appoint one dedicated executive, one whose only objective is to rethink and challenge our current way of thinking, that can make all the difference. I believe that this is probably the best alternative to falling into a short-term, instead of a long-term perspective. Innovation is a journey, but there has to be someone, or a group of people, designated with the sponsorship of the board. We should also consider that the opportunities associated with innovation shouldn't be restricted to fit into the current company structure. Innovation could have massive implications on the current executive team and that alone would allow for crucial innovation falling outside of scope because it can mean large parts of the company will become redundant, including executive team members. This is the reason the innovation head and team must have sponsors on the board.

The innovation owner is not the only person who is responsible. He or she has to orchestrate changes with the support of Human Resources. In fact, I see the role of HR as needing to change from recruiting and retrenching, or operational efforts, to developing and adjusting the organization to remain competitive. The HR management role is going through the same transition as the CFO role, moving from a bookkeeper into a strategic role. HR managers should be change agents through recruiting or education, and help the team relearn on the journey.

When we measure the success of innovation, I believe that if you cannot transfer the benefits of innovation into economic or social value, then it will be too difficult to define the success or, for that matter, to give credit for the innovation and inspire and motivate others to change.

One success factor I recently used was to launch new products where the success criteria were to reach one million subscribers. Anything less was considered a failure. That forced the team to adopt a mindset where they asked, "How can we become 10 times bigger?" or "How can we become 100 times bigger?" The large scale of the challenge forced us to build each product with an ambitious goal in mind from the start. It also meant that other internal projects could compete for our customers. This was very healthy, because you need a well-defined competitor to fight against in order to thrive. We were very successful at creating a productive competitive environment within our own organization.

The products competed amongst each other in order to reach the one million by maximizing ease of use. Remember, going from 0 to 1 million is a significant increase. There are so many products and services that reach 10 or 100 subscribers and then in three months' time, someone has copied it and the subscription growth rate declines. Finally, we had maybe 100 or 200 products and services. What was difficult was making the decision to pull the plug on the unsuccessful ones. We found ourselves paying the costs and employing at least 4 or 5 people to keep each product running year over year because we were not allowing them to fail fast enough.

I believe in employing strategic leadership and innovation within any finance function for which I've been responsible. We should spend less time on business as usual and much more time on strategic thinking and innovation. Otherwise, all companies and businesses are bound to lose. Everyone realizes this, but many shy away from addressing the problem head on. The more time you spend on business-as-usual activities, the more likely someone is going to come along and take your business or your customers.

There is often a tendency to be risk averse in big companies because failure can cause great trouble for you and the company. You can lose your job or your career can be adversely affected. Yet failure is an integral part of innovation. It is crucial to address this conundrum. Failure has many faces. It is easy to claim that you should expect to fail a lot and do it fast, but when you do fail are you able to identify what has happened as a failure? In large, rich companies that is not so easy. A lot of time and energy is invested and prestige is involved as well. In fact, not identifying a failure is a failure in and of itself. In my experience, that can be a significant long-term cost.

The person leading a project is hardly in a position to question success v. failure for themselves. Someone from the outside has to question each project and their proposed innovations. To identify which innovations are failures and which deserve further investment should not be the job of the individuals tasked with innovating. In some of the cases we have seen, one alternative is to separate those responsible for innovation and put them away from the big organization. They are given the opportunity to come into the company and challenge it from the inside without bureaucracy, with the only task being to break the company faster than the competition. Do things smarter, faster, and cheaper and also find completely different things to offer to the market.

So, what shall we do when people fail? We must pick them up. Usually we celebrate successes while failures fade away in isolation. How do you celebrate and pick up the people who failed? Here, one of the problems is incentives. There are people who are working on the day-to-day operations and there are people working on the innovation side. Failures are very difficult to incentivize, but, perhaps, so are successes. What is a success and what happens after it? It is often the case that when an innovator has reached a success point, there's no incentive plan attached. What happens next? You risk losing those people, the really quality people, to other companies. They might even leave to run their own companies.

Innovation to decrease cost is usually fairly easy to measure and incentivize. You can measure the economic waste you eradicate and get paid a percentage. That kind of incentive program has been very successful and is easy to implement.

But I still haven't answered the question of how we incentivize failure. The easiest way may be to recognize the failure and assign more resources for another try with undamaged confidence. You should set up metrics that ensure the project still makes sense and determine that the failure did not result from of lack of imagination or hard work. It is easy to fail and you must prove that you tried to do the best you could. If you don't try hard enough that shouldn't be enough to earn you any recognition, but if you did all that was humanly possible, and really explored all the opportunities and never gave up, that should be considered a 'good' failure. Be sure to capture the lessons learned from the failure so you can take a step up and continue on a higher level for the next attempt.

One way to incentivize good failures can be to open up a competition, saying that the best failure this year (for example) receives a prize of some sort. You have to have judges and criteria that everyone knows about in advance and that are fair and sensible. We have to be clear of when to call it quits, when we must admit that we have failed. It should not be too early and not too late. The failure, and, more importantly, the attitude of really trying and succeeding, could then serve as a role model taking away the stigma of failure in the organization.

Another area where the CFO can support innovation is in the supply chain. Currently, the models to introduce innovation in big companies are often different than the models small companies use. Innovation is more natural for many small companies in your supply chain. They have to be innovative in order to survive. Many are run by a single entrepreneur and the whole organization is very close to their customers. The small company lives and breathes innovation. They know how to handle failures, but they usually have hard restrictions in the form of available cash. When they try to take on large challenges, they are forced to innovate more narrowly and not in a blue sky fashion.

In the meantime, the CFOs of large companies in the supply chain are often incentivized to decrease working capital – meaning they push payment terms onto the weaker suppliers and distributors in their network. Besides increasing the risk for supply chain disruptions, this also forces the small suppliers to restrict the efforts they put into innovation. If the small innovative companies in the supply chain decrease their contributions to innovation, it effectively means that they must outsource the major innovation efforts to large, less flexible companies, which often have a less innovative DNA.

This is an effect of the working capital targets we rarely discuss. The more reluctant small ecosystem participants are to participate, the less innovative the whole sector is. Financing the supply chain is no different than the blood within the circulatory system. It has to be clean and pump in sufficient volumes. That makes your body healthier, and when your whole body is healthy, your brain functions much better. We must take a full ecosystem view and for that perspective, I believe the supply chain, the banking community, and the big corporates should transfer the outstanding financial strengths onto the smaller companies within their ecosystems.

I believe they can do it through using current systems, but processes should be more straightforward. Clearly most large corporates have lots of credit lines which are not used because they are not productive or they don't have any projects. They have to let the 'fresh blood' into the supply chain by releasing those resources.

Together with the banks, the large corporates have to actively disperse working capital to where it is needed. The banks need the corporations to guide them into their ecosystem of suppliers and distributors. They need to cooperate to develop the best solutions. The purpose should be that all players in the ecosystem actively participate in innovation for the good of the whole system. When that happens, the risk of obsolescence and disruption decreases, which also is good for the banks.

The CFO needs to be very active here, I believe. The funding situation can change dramatically and very quickly. We saw this in 2008–2010 and we'll see it again. The CFO has the responsibility to ensure that there is always sufficient funding everywhere in the whole supply chain and to ensure that innovation comes in return. The funding strategy needs to have a holistic perspective and focus on the long-term survival and optimization of the ecosystem.

I believe that there are many new solutions out there that will help us introduce abilities for better transparency and tracking of funds. This is an area where we can improve an awful lot. I think combining clever credit scoring, risk management techniques, and facilitated communications will be with us soon. Technological innovation will happen quickly in this space. You can already leverage your ecosystem for supply chain financing, for instance, without using your own cash. You don't even need to use your own balance sheet.

For the policy makers, the problem is that the money is already in the economy but it's not transforming into investments, jobs, or growth. Most of the printed money ends up being conservatively invested with the focus on preserving its own value. The ecosystem cooperation I've been talking about can be the missing link to get the economy going again. I doubt zero percent interest rates will do the trick.

The fact that the small innovative companies don't have the funds to innovate is a consequence, not a root cause problem in and of itself. The real problem is that money cannot find the right direction because the supply chains are not sufficiently cooperative. They contain a mix of separate entities without a common goal. We need to change that to ensure creative thinking and innovation expanding fast enough to fuel competitive advantage.

Conclusion

Murat Erden is explicit about the fact that finance does not work in isolation. He even puts the CFO in the driver's seat of innovation and business development in order to ensure the survival of the whole company. He sees the company as one single unit and renounces the concept of silos.

Murat focuses on how companies can remain competitive, disrupting themselves faster than their competitors, and thereby surviving longer. This is definitely a customer-centric orientation, since survival requires the company to satisfy their customers' needs and wants.

Murat drives his organization to excel by providing clear targets for his team, delegating responsibility, and focusing on results – thereby challenging functional silos. He also dares to advance discussions on a lateral level instead of a functional one, serving as a natural catalyst for a process flow perspective.

Innovation is at the top of his agenda and he doesn't allow himself to be distracted by the 'not-invented-here' syndrome. Murat is focused on beating the competition; where innovation comes from is less important. He states that it is better for a company to disrupt itself than to rely upon competitors to provide incentives. He mentions supply chain finance as a good opportunity and alludes to large cash-rich companies taking a whole supply chain perspective and taking responsibility for allocating capital and risk optimally over the supply chain. He acknowledges that small companies usually have more innovative DNA than large multinationals – a fact that no ambitious leadership team can overlook.

Key Take-Aways

- Finance must focus on making a significant difference to the company's business and support its survival over the long term.
- Innovation, though desirable, is not a natural output of executive leadership teams – especially at large, established firms. In order to ensure that it is assigned the appropriate priority and resources, someone must own innovation just as other leaders own HR, IT, finance, and marketing.

- When innovation is a shared responsibility in the executive team, it will drown in the day-to-day operations.
- In addition to being prized, albeit hard to foster, innovation requires enough risk-taking that it does not always thrive in an environment that abhors failure.
- Innovation does not spring forth from positions of comfort, but in response to pressure and/or friction.
- The role of HR is to nurture and develop an innovation mindset throughout the company.
- Although they may seem intangible, the benefits of innovation must be clearly measurable.
- Fast failure is healthier (and more efficient) than lingering uncertainty and downward trending performance.
- The way in which successes and failures are incentivized is critical to determining which will win out; the stigma of failure must be renounced.
- Define the criteria for innovation success and failure early on – and stick to it.

Murat Erden was the EVP and CFO of Turkcell from 2012 until 2016, which he joined as Treasury Director in 2001. During this period, he was in charge of the financial management of the Turkcell Group which operates in nine countries. Turkcell was one of the five companies with the highest market capitalization in Turkey and is one of the top 500 companies listed on the NYSE. He was named as one of "50 CFOs to Watch" by the Global Telecoms Business in both 2015 and 2016. He was also named among the 50 most influential CFOs in Turkey across all industries by *Fortune Magazine* in 2016. In May 2016 Murat relocated to London, UK where he established his own consultancy firm. In June 2017, he joined an international telecom company in London.

8

Nudging the Financial Supply Chain

David Loseby

Summary

The rationale behind the adoption of any given framework can easily be assumed to be based on logic and reason. For execution, however, we must be prepared to understand and accommodate more emotionally driven behavioral effects. While the financial supply chain may be a conduit for currency and cash, it is still subject to the whims and imperfections of the human beings in charge. For that reason, investments in the relationships between supply partners of varying sizes and structures are as critical to customer value and profitability as any other organizational effort.

David provides the following definition for Behavioral Procurement:

Behavioral Procurement (BP) and the related field of Behavioral Economics (BE) study the effects of psychological, social, cognitive, and emotional factors on the commercial decisions of individuals and institutions and the consequences for competitive advantage, innovation and resource allocation. BP is primarily concerned with bounds of rationality of commercial agents and factors. BP models typically integrate insights from BE, psychology, decision sciences, social sciences, and market theory, as well as implicitly nudging; in so doing, these behavioral models cover a range of concepts methods and fields.

As a result of the above explanation, the associated training and development are likely to focus on the following key areas:

D. Loseby
Inchcape plc., London, UK

© The Author(s) 2018
M. Lind, K. Barner, *Finance Unleashed*, DOI 10.1007/978-3-319-66370-8_8

- Organizational behaviors and their impact.
- Avoidance mechanisms for buyer/supplier stress.
- Relationship lifecycle management.
- Decision architecture.
- 'Nudging' or achieving a desired direction by consensus or policy adoption without the loss of transparency.

In this chapter, David explains why it is so important to take a behavioral approach to procurement – especially in the context of the financial supply chain.

Interview with David Loseby conducted July 5, 2016

Several other functions besides procurement are exploring the potential of behavioral interventions. Behavioral finance has already been established and is parallel to behavioral economics. The people in marketing and sales have been using some of the elements of behavioral economics in the way in which they've done things, particularly in terms of 'nudging' or pushing a behavior gently and gradually in the desired direction.

Governments have done it too. In the USA and the UK, in particular, governments are using what is sometimes called a 'behavioral insights team' to help shape and form policies. So the application of behavioral studies in procurement can hardly be new news.

I recently gave a keynote to members of the marketing community. They said, "Wow, the competition is now really on because if procurement is going to get ahold of behavioral economics then the game's up for us!" It's quite interesting that they realized that we can take the lessons learned and apply them in different ways. They suddenly recognized that this different way of doing business, shows that they had all to themselves for so long, suddenly this was no longer going to be reserved for marketing alone.

My PhD is focused around the behavioral sciences, which encompass psychology, social science, and decision science. It is built upon the principles established in behavioral economics, and by applying the parallel, into procurement too. It includes all the different branches, such as supplier relationship management, supply chain finance, risk management, contract management – all the things that are involved in the broader spectrum of procurement as a discipline.

How can we relate Behavioral Procurement to supply chain management? And in particular to the financial supply chain?

Well, I think the connection is in looking at how you can manage the risks, and risks come in lots of different formats and from different directions. A risk could be anything from a physical risk to a financial risk to a political risk, etc. We look at all those aspects in theory, but also at the way in which a lot of things actually work. One good example of this is the 2016 Brexit vote [where 52 percent of Britons cast a vote to leave the European Union]. The actual result of the referendum deviated largely from the advance polls, most of which had projected a 'remain' [in the EU] outcome.

So, how did this happen? When we approach a choice, we expect logic and rationale to rule, when the reality is that all of the votes were cast on the basis of emotions, behaviors, and experiences – a dynamic that can be explained by Prospect Theory, developed by two professors, Kahneman and Tversky, in the late 1970s. The polling institutions forgot to include all the emotional and behavioral aspects of the voter decision-making process. In the same way, when people are making economic predictions, the construction of the model itself may get in the way of an accurate result because traditional economic models are based primarily upon linear projections and rationale.

The reality is that more often than not people make big decisions not just based upon what I call 'hard rationale and facts,' but also include a level of behavioral and other emotional and experiential components.

How would that model apply to engaging the entire ecosystem involved in one demand and supply chain? If we want to introduce a whole interconnected chain we must be able to make people feel related to each other. How should they cooperate, for instance? The relationship between the buyer and seller is usually a bit strained because there are reasons not to be completely transparent. For instance, a supplier tries not to say to the buyer that his company has scarce liquidity, because he is concerned that the buyer might be concerned about having a financially shaky supplier. How do you create a relationship of trust in an ecosystem that naturally includes both shared and independent incentives?

We need to accept that relationships are not linear. I think this is where being able to define at what point in the supply chain you might want to improve working capital, liquidity, and all of those things is a key step. I believe that once you have established a relationship – after going through a competitive process to select the supplier and put proper contracts in place – from this point onwards, the relationship development phase starts. That is where most of the value is actually created, as opposed to during the Request for Proposal (RFP) process. At this point, we should be looking at how we can optimize processes, innovation, cash flow, investments, risk management, and working capital.

You can compare it with how General Motors and Toyota handled their supplier relationships ten years ago. General Motors was renowned for its supplier 'bullying' while Toyota chose to support and invest in their suppliers, which turned out to be the most profitable approach in the long run.

You know a company has the wrong focus when they think they're being very smart in how they conduct business but their approach is actually costing them more money. Even having a sufficient understanding of how suppliers' markets work can make a huge difference in a company's ability to work with them. By putting a proposal on the table right from the outset and saying, "We will work with you to develop supply chain finance solutions combined with management strategies, corporate social responsibility efforts, and more". In my opinion, this is about procurement becoming more sophisticated and mature as a function. I think that's what some of the more successful organizations are doing, albeit it requires a different level of skill and competence to do that.

In a manner of speaking, the aim of the PhD is to structure and model frameworks that allow organizations to become more emotional or empathetic. What we're trying to do is to avoid putting into place what I call 'rigid' rules, systems, and processes. It's more about building frameworks and competencies – both of which are critical to how procurement works. In fact, this takes us back to the roots of Behavioral Procurement where one size most certainly does not fit all. If you're going to develop a Supply Chain Finance program, for example, you'll have to have a variety of frameworks that allow different segment sizes and corresponding mechanisms for each to leverage the program. If you don't, you're going back to the traditional banking system which is 'it's our way or no way' – being one reason that has blocked and complicated access to currency and cash throughout the value chain.

Say you are working in a big company. You have your first tier of suppliers and then you want that level of suppliers to work in the same way with the second tier and then the third tier and so forth. How do you create an ecosystem that includes all tiers equally, regardless of their proximity? Do you create some kind of behavioral ecosystem or will it be only those that are closely surrounding us that benefits from this?

What you could create is actually more of a behavioral support structure. Rather than simply dictating what you want, you should consider making it accessible and easy to understand. Typically, you will find this where you've got suppliers or supply chains with intrinsic value to the company, ideally leading to innovation and competitive advantage. This is not the sort of thing that you would expect to find within the manufacturing space, where common component parts can be supplied by a multitude of suppliers.

In some ways, you actually step away from the supplier you're contracting with to manage its supply chain because it is the design piece of what they provide that is in essence what you're buying from the company. Breaking into a supplier's supply chain to access the second or third tier may disrupt their ability to innovate.

The preferred approach is to incentivize tier one and tier two providers to dig into their own supply chains. I think that is more appropriate because you'll have some companies that are cash-poor and others that are cash-rich. You have to make a support provision available and accessible and then leave the company to decide which path they need support, be it finance or otherwise. Letting people decide which fit is most appropriate for their business and vision ensures that the cost of finance will be determined by a number of different factors. Businesses need to piece out the more different parts of their business to finance, because the things that are financially toxic either won't get financed or will be deemed too expensive and unlikely to be of real advantage to the business.

To truly work, I think you have to have more emphasis on business relationship management that goes alongside new financing options and approaches, because financing is often not what is missing from a traditional bank.

In 2016, American Express did a study of 250 small and medium-sized businesses in Australia that failed to invest enough in innovation.[1] Their reasons included both an inability to develop innovation and research plans as challenges around securing funding. The effect was that the large companies had to accept a disproportionate amount of the innovation efforts and costs.

This is often a problem. We know that the primary issue with the whole process of design and piloting and bringing a new product or innovation to market is that it is very, very costly, and that it is often not the area where banks want to invest. Innovation and research are the lifeblood of the supply chain. More often than not, they are only funded by businesses with sufficient profits to be able to make those investments in their future.

If Supply Chain Finance is really going to take off, then there has to be a way of finding solutions to some of those sorts of problems. That's where I think you will see a massive step change in the way in which financing is provided.

When it's an issue of innovation, you need to steer so the money is flowing down in a timely fashion and directed into innovation. The funding and steering have to be maintained through many tiers, even into the smallest companies because they are often more agile. If you think about it in procurement terms, you talk about the same ability and need for ethical procurement as before.

Back to the previous point again, though, this is about making sure that the capital gets into the right hands quickly so that you can free up the cash flow of those investments in innovation. That value is what will make businesses very healthy and eventually the whole economy healthy.

Finally, you may discuss how the current rate of disruption in most industries is picking up in pace because the strength of the large incumbents often lies in the brand and the global organization. Many incumbents are currently being unbundled by start-ups who use social media to build a brand and the Internet to sell directly instead of through large sales organizations or distributors. Large incumbents risk death by a thousand cuts. One line of defense for these companies could be to leverage the innovation capabilities of their own supply base.

This is why operating models based upon behavioral science as opposed to rigid, traditional structures and linear thinking can be superior for the incumbents. This is where the excitement is, and that's where the sort of benefit you can start to accrue stems from. The challenge remains in linear behavior that forces us to say, "We'll be happy to structure this part of the business or that subsidiary this way but you need to see proof that it will work." If, instead, you can approach it in a 'behavioral' way that is transparent and measurable and structured you could create a different operating model altogether. That's what we need to get our heads around.

Conclusion

David Loesby approaches the isolation of finance from the perspective of a Chief Procurement Officer (CPO). As such, he would often find himself as a part of the CFO's office, yet without being a finance professional per se (which proves the CFO's office is built up with disparate departments). One advantage a CPO can provide in a CFO's office is to connect finance to external stakeholders (suppliers) in the physical chain and thus provide the external perspective. A CPO can serve as a catalyst to bring finance out of isolation.

The CPO is naturally supplier-centric and can translate procurement's models and thinking to the demand side. Many CPOs would benefit from including the demand chain in their purview. The CPO and supply chain managers in the CFO's office can act as subject matter experts when transferring process optimization techniques from the physical to the financial chain. When David introduces a behavioral approach to cooperation he adds a new dimension; interaction that can be applied to the entire supply chain.

The behavioral way to approach supply chain cooperation is invigorating since it can induce the cooperation required to innovate. When large, cash-rich companies are trying to inject innovation into their supply chains, they should focus on nimbler entities that are better at innovation. With a behavioral mindset, large companies can provide valuable support and input to the supply chain. Suppliers should be left to pursue innovation on their own – including the management of their own supply chain. This opens up the possibility for cooperation over several tiers into the supply and demand chain. Behavioral mindsets invite the supply chain into closer cooperation by sharing an agreed-upon set of behaviors as a 'soft' version of vertical integration.

Key Take-Aways

- The traditional framework of 'people, process, and technology' is typically applied with the assumption that talent will be the focus of the 'people' dimension. While this may be logical for some applications, it overlooks the behavioral impact that talent can have on processes and results.

- Policies may be based on logic and reason, but in an operational setting human reactions and imperfections can lead to unexpected results.
- When organizations are rolling out frameworks of any kind, they must strike a balance between enough structure to achieve consistency and limit error, but not so much that the potential for value is constrained.
- Decisions, even professional decisions, are influenced by subjective and emotional factors. How do we ensure our decisions create the desired outcomes?
- The relationship-building process between buyer and supplier contains the majority of the value created by a contract, although it cannot begin until the competitive bidding process is over.
- Creating positive behaviors and allowing for local decision making authority will provide better results than rigid one-size-fits-all models in procurement.
- Behavioral finance and behavioral procurement are disciplines the CFO office can use to instill desired behaviors without having to uphold strict rules and policies.

Note

1. "Opportunity for Innovation Highlighted by 2016 American Express CFO Future-Proofing Survey," *PASA*, June 2, 2016, http://procurementandsupply. com/2016/06/opportunity-innovation-highlighted-2016-american-express-cfo-future-proofing-survey/.

David Loseby currently the Chief Procurement Officer at Inchcape, has more than 25 years' experience as a senior executive, driving organizational transformation through procurement. David is also working on research to earn his PhD, focusing on "Behavioral Procurement", a concept that runs parallel to the related field of Behavioral Economics.

9

Leadership Is Not Enough

Adrian Atkinson

Summary

Companies are conditioned to prize leadership and influence in their employees – particularly when it comes to executive-level responsibility and promotion. Yet even the best leaders often do not generate the kinds of operational results that the company wants to see. Based on his research with thousands of talented professionals, Dr. Adrian Atkinson has identified a rare type of person that he calls a 'Wealth Creator'. Roughly 2 percent of the population of senior managers and executives are Wealth Creators. Contrary to what you might expect, Wealth Creators are often not natural leaders or even in leadership roles and may have trouble getting along with managers and colleagues. Put them in the right position, however, and give them the right support and they can significantly change a company's direction for the better. In his contribution, Adrian sheds light on who Wealth Creators are and what wealth creation means.

Interview with Adrian Atkinson conducted August 17, 2016

I started to work on the concept of Wealth Creators in 2009. The issue for me was that while I knew that many of the people we coached were good leaders, they didn't really drive the business. I also noticed that we had assessed some people who actually did drive business and created significant wealth. The question was, "How are they doing that? Are they doing something more than people who are just good leaders?"

A. Atkinson
Human Factors International, London, UK

© The Author(s) 2018
M. Lind, K. Barner, *Finance Unleashed*, DOI 10.1007/978-3-319-66370-8_9

To study this further I identified 20 people that I knew personally, people we had assessed and who created enormous wealth for their company in a very short space of time. I reviewed all the assessments that we had done and found that they all fell into a pattern. That pattern is now what we use to identify Wealth Creators.

Wealth Creators are the people who consistently drive business in the short and long term. They significantly increase the value of the business in a sustainable way. An analogy I use is of the yeast in a loaf of bread. It is a small, but crucial ingredient that creates lots of difference. Without the yeast you will get a completely different loaf of bread, but the yeast needs all the other ingredients as well. You cannot have a loaf just made of yeast!

Another analogy I use is the striker in a football [i.e., soccer] team. The striker is the person who scores most of the goals, and that's what the Wealth Creator is. The striker needs all the other people on the football team to back him or her up and to support the opportunities for scoring goals, but if you don't have strikers, you don't score the goals that you need to win. You might still score a few goals, but not the ones that win you all the games.

So, we're looking at those people who drive the business and who make it extraordinarily successful. What we see are seven characteristics. These people are *analytical and intellectually able*. They are *energetic* and *proactive*. They are *resilient to pressure*, you might even say they thrive on pressure. They are *open to ideas, competitive* and *confident*. These are the characteristics we assess to identify Wealth Creators.

When we reviewed the 2,072 profiles we had of executives and senior managers, only 39 – or a strikingly low 2 percent – were Wealth Creators. This means that only one in every 53 leaders was also a Wealth Creator. That percentage has less to do with our sample and more to do with the fact that these people are rare. What is also very interesting is that there was hardly any gender difference. In the 1590 male profiles we reviewed, there were 29 Wealth Creators (1.8 percent, or 1 in 55). In the 482 female profiles we reviewed, there were 10 Wealth Creators (2.1 percent, or 1 in 48). So you get about the same number of females as males.

Should the Wealth Creator be a CEO?

We have identified Wealth Creators who are CEOs of large companies and of small companies. We identified Wealth Creators who are CFOs. We identified a Wealth Creator who is a group commercial director. We have some Wealth Creators who are further down in the organization and who are just coming up.

The problem that up-and-coming Wealth Creators experience is that their colleagues, who are not Wealth Creators, tend to find them very pushy. They find them very difficult to get on with because they are always so energetic, driving to make things happen and to move everybody forward – not always in the direction that others want to go. Consequently, some of their colleagues find them difficult to talk to or to work with on projects. Wealth

Creators don't have a lot of patience and are always driving to make progress. The Wealth Creator finds it difficult to work with people who don't go along with what they're saying and who have no good reason for disagreeing with them. One of the things we do is coach Wealth Creators to be more influential with people and not so straightforward and direct.

Is it a challenge to manage a Wealth Creator? There might be a risk that they will isolate themselves if they behave in this pushy manner and then they don't really leverage their gift. Wealth Creators can isolate themselves if they just carry on the way they want to. The company needs to identify them, manage them, and support them. We need to give their colleagues an understanding of how to manage and work with them because they've got to be recognized as something really special. They may not be easy to get on with, but they are fantastic in an organization. They make all the difference. They will frequently have a flaw. They will frequently have particular traits that irritate many. They are not perfect people, they're not Super men and women.

Once we have identified that someone is a Wealth Creator we then look for their flaw (or flaws!). This may be an exceptional speed of thinking, leaving others behind – interpersonal characteristics that make it difficult for them to get on with people. In doing this, we are able to coach the Wealth Creator to be a little bit better at linking with other people and also coach the team around them to be more effective in using their strengths.

So, how do we identify the Wealth Creators? Imagine you have a company with 5,000 people. It sounds as if it may be a trial and error, or a lottery for you to go in and find them, like finding the needle in a haystack. Yes, it can be tricky and when one of our clients recognizes people as being difficult to get on with, very pushy, determined, and yet adding good value for the company at the same time, they ask us to assess them. They ask us, "Are these Wealth Creators, is that what the issue is here?" Sometimes it is, and sometimes it isn't. Our way is usually to do a management and executive screening audit then we can objectively identify the people who are likely to be Wealth Creators. Once we've shortlisted the potential Wealth Creators we do a full assessment of them. This identifies exactly what the organization has in terms of Wealth Creators.

They can be anywhere, in junior or senior positions, and they can be harder to find if they haven't reached the executive level yet. We start off by identifying the ones who are likely to be Wealth Creators and then we give them the full assessment. It's very straightforward and it renders great results.

You might expect Wealth Creators to be entrepreneurs and start their own companies, yet very few of them are entrepreneurs. Genuine entrepreneurs are even rarer than Wealth Creators. Wealth Creators will take risks, but not excessive risks. Entrepreneurs take excessive risks. Only some entrepreneurs are also Wealth Creators.

We have identified four types of Wealth Creators, people who are:

* Expert
* Corporate
* Enterpriser
* Entrepreneurial

So we've got four different types of Wealth Creators. When you can not only identify whether someone is a Wealth Creator, but also what type of Wealth Creator they are, you realize how to make the most of these people. The Expert Wealth Creator has the lowest level of risk taking and the Entrepreneurial Wealth Creator has the highest level of risk taking.

This book discusses the changing role of the CFO to not only be the vanguard of financial stability, but also to develop the business and find new revenue streams. What does this mean to the CFO, because generally there are a few CFOs who are Wealth Creators. How could they fit in as a CFO?

The Wealth Creator CFO takes a wider approach to the business than the usual functional approach. They're always looking at how the rest of the organization works. CFOs who just stay as financial people, within their own functional group, can be superb as financial officers, but they are not going to be Wealth Creators. They are not thinking in terms of the wider strategic context of being a business driver. Wealth Creators think of being a business driver first and a CFO second.

For a typical accounting-type CFO, what would he or she do to become a strategic CFO or business-oriented CFO? The answer is, it depends on the characteristics of the individual. We need a full assessment to give us a full understanding of their key strengths, key limitations, and potential.

We assessed and interviewed a finance director who is looking to become the group finance director. His issue is that he's not thinking like an executive. He is not thinking wide enough for the organization. This is fairly typical of finance people, who tend to stick to their functional area. Wealth Creators don't do that, even when they are low down in the organization. They're always interacting with and listening to and looking at what the rest of the organization is doing, and saying, "How can we do things better together and how do we make it happen quickly?"

Sometimes you have to be a bit patient. I know someone who was a finance director and he wanted to become an operational director. The company wouldn't support him because they said he didn't have enough experience. We assessed him and we said, "Well, he's even better than that. He's a Wealth

Creator, and so he could be the CEO of this subsidiary of yours." They didn't like the idea because of his lack of experience. So he left the organization and became the group CFO for a much larger company. Not only that, he's now going to be made CEO of that larger company. The route a Wealth Creator takes is usually through functions and then they quickly come into a more general management role and then often make it to being a CEO.

We are often asked if you can train someone to become a Wealth Creator, or if you must be born into it. The fact of the matter is that people develop to become Wealth Creators from quite an early age. A bit like entrepreneurs, they develop at a young age into being a Wealth Creator. By the age of 25–30, you can tell if they are going to be a Wealth Creator or not. We have found potential Wealth Creators at the age of 27 in junior positions. We have recommended that they should be promoted to a senior job very quickly. One company I know refused to do that and the guy left after two years and started his own business, which was far more successful than the one he had left.

Another person was about 28 years of age. His boss asked us, "Can you assess and coach him? Otherwise I'm going to sack him. He's such a difficult person." So we said, "Okay, we'll assess him." He turned out to be a Wealth Creator, and we said "Move him away from you because he's not getting on with you. Give him to the CEO to be his strategy analyst." The CEO listened, trusted us, did that, and the company increased its value exponentially over the next five years. You can be a Wealth Creator quite young – you don't have to wait. You develop the characteristics of the Wealth Creator at about the age of 25–30.

Conclusion

Adrian discusses Wealth Creators and addresses this point directly: "...So CFOs who just stay as financial people, within their own functional group, can be superb as financial officers, but they are not going to be Wealth Creators because they are not thinking in terms of the wider context of being a business driver. Wealth Creators think of being a business driver first and a CFO second."

The creation of value for customers and wealth for shareholders are the key reasons for operating a company. Consequently, finding and nurturing the yeast in the bread – or the scarcely found Wealth Creator – is a key to astounding success.

Key Take-Aways

- Corporations reward leadership, responsibility, and hard work. These highly prized traits may not lead to exceptional wealth creation.
- Leaders are not necessarily Wealth Creators.
- Wealth Creators represent just 2 percent of the management population and there is hardly any gender difference.
- Wealth Creators are not functionally siloed.
- Wealth Creators are: analytical and intellectually able; energetic and proactive; able to thrive under pressure; open to ideas; competitive and confident.
- Wealth Creators are often hard to handle and can be sidestepped.
- Wealth Creators need their colleagues to support their unusual ideas.
- Wealth Creators are determined, pushy, and driven. By identifying these people and providing a supportive framework, their talents for growing the business can be realized.
- There are four types of Wealth Creator: the Expert; the Corporate; the Enterpriser; and the Entrepreneur.
- Identify not only who your Wealth Creators are, but also what type they are, and then you will be winning!

Adrian Atkinson is a Chartered Psychologist with over 30 years' experience as an international business consultant and executive coach. He assists organizations to be highly effective by assessing and developing key players and integrating their HR strategies with corporate objectives. Adrian has carried out national, multinational, and government consultancy assignments in the UK, Europe, Asia-Pacific, India, and the USA. He has coached senior executives in several FTSE 100 companies. He has contributed to numerous radio and TV programs, notably BBC's 'Mind of the Millionaire', and has specialist expertise in leadership, business strategy, and *wealth creation*.

10

Let Them Eat Cake

Peter Huber

Summary

Every function in the organization must tie their focus, objectives, and performance metrics to customer satisfaction. Unfortunately, many companies take a myopic internal focus that leads them to focus more on their internal activities and processes than on how their efforts create customer value. As Peter Huber explains, not adopting a customer-centric view is naïve, foolish, and dangerous. He refers to himself as the 'customers' best friend', even after a career in production and supply chain management (and not in sales). He also talks about 'customer-centricity'. Here he tells us what he means by the term.

Interview with Peter Huber conducted July 3, 2016

Customer centricity, at least from a financial supply chain perspective, is all about breaking down organizational silos. Having a mature leadership team driving the customer-centric effort requires a CEO and a very good management team that keep customers at the center of the corporate agenda.

There is only one customer. We should not have any 'internal' customers. There is only one customer and that is the person who actually buys our product, is hopefully happy with our services, and would like to return to us again. That is the person who pays our salaries. Every time we need a new system or some new people, that bill is going to be paid for by the customer, because the company still has to look out for their bottom line, even when operating costs go up.

P. Huber
IKEA, Malmö, Sweden

© The Author(s) 2018
M. Lind, K. Barner, *Finance Unleashed*, DOI 10.1007/978-3-319-66370-8_10

Ironically, it is easier to speak about the lack of customer-centricity seen in many organizations. Many times, management teams are driven by an inside-out perspective rather than an outside-in perspective. The customer's voice can be drowned out by meetings full of subject matter experts. The outside-in representatives, if there are any, are usually drowned out by the pressure to advance an internally focused agenda.

The voice of the customer is seldom heard because at the top of the agenda you will find finance and someone from production. At best you might have a sales representative there, speaking a little bit about customers. Then people get tired, break up for a cup of coffee, and move on to discussing the latest IT topic. While each function thinks about what they can do to improve, they often fail to make the connection between their objectives and actions and their responsibility to deliver something of value to the customer.

If you want to invest in something to increase the speed of customer acquisition or the level of customer retention, you are more likely to find discussions within the company about who is going to pay the bill than what it means for the customer. Rather than focusing on what we can do to get a solution in place to help the customer, we talk about the cost and implementation effort. We are naturally problem-oriented rather than solution or value-oriented. I have observed this trend in many areas, particularly in the financial sector where I have seen very little customer-centricity at all.

The fundamental reason for this lack of customer focus or inside-out perspective boils down to two things: firstly, the corporate culture and secondly, the behavior or leadership style. These are directly linked to the management team and implementation and changes need to come down from the top. There are no quick fixes (other than boldness) and each executive must start with 'the man in the mirror'.

To create a customer-centric view in a company, especially within the finance function, you need a lot of small activities that have to come together to lead to the right view. It must start from the top down. You need to have a CEO with a consistent customer-centric mindset. It doesn't mean that he or she should not also focus on traditional business support-related issues. Even support-related issues must have a customer-centric focus. After the CEO, we must have the same expectations of the CFO. Having a mature, cohesive leadership team breaking down functional silos brings together the whole value chain in a way that each person focusing on their specific segment of the business will not.

One of my core messages is that companies often have too many voices representing the inside-out view and not enough representing the outside-in. Why is making sure that the second perspective is heard so important? It sounds like it creates the need for a balance between internal process improvements and selling – the perspective that traditionally represents the customer on the executive team.

Process improvements have value if they allow you to have a better P&L, a better profit, and so on. But that value is only real if customers feel that your improvement has a meaning in the form of good prices, superior product quality, exceptional service levels, etc. Then process improvements can be seen for the customer's sake. The worst-case scenario is when our focus on internal processes eclipses our view of the customer; we can sometimes even miss deadlines that we have promised to customers because we are fighting each other over internal issues.

Say you sit in a management meeting and the managing director, or whoever happens to be leading it, opens up and says, "Let's hear what's happening in the production area." And the production lead responds by saying, "Well, we have this level of allocation. We need some more resources there, and needs over here. Also, we need to buy a new machine." And then the director asks the same of HR and they say, "We have three people too few here, five people are redundant, and we absolutely must bring in this new kind of training."

And then the sales director says, "We have 250,000 prospects. We have short-listed them and so on and so forth." And then it's time for finance who says, "This is the current P&L and balance sheet."

This kind of discussion is as far from the customer perspective as you can get. I would address this situation by standing up and say, "You're all naïve, foolish, and dangerous." Those would be my first words to them.

They are *naïve* because they believe the organization knows how it is doing without focusing on the customer or business development. They are *foolish* because they don't realize they are considered non-value add by the customers. Finally, they are *dangerous* because they are too distant from the customer. They have no relationship with their end-users, and as a result they can't verbalize the company's benefit to them.

Let me give you another example. If we continue to go around the hypothetical management meeting table and the next person is from procurement and says, "These are my savings for this month. We have cut out 2 or 3 percent on the P&L." He would be pronounced a hero by everyone in the room.

This is a real, live example because it was actually me who said those words. What happened, one month later, however, was that our delivery performance went down because we had squeezed our suppliers so hard on the price that they were unable to deliver in full. The goods weren't the same high quality we were used to. We completely forgot the big picture because we were so focused on the lowest price rather than on the lowest cost.

The same lesson can be found in HR when they are discussing the high costs of sick leave. There is not necessarily anything wrong with this – sick leave costs can be a good KPI [Key Performance Indicator] or measurement – but you should measure its impact on the customer, saying, "How does this affect my output?" If you have a person missing, whether in the long or short-term, it's not the cost of replacing that person that truly matters. The question we should be asking and answering is, "What will this cost us in terms of our output?" We need to understand how sick leave will affect our ability to deliver a quality solution to the customer. Perhaps our short-term staffing solution ultimately makes us too expensive? Every measurement must be discussed in terms of how it translates to the customer experience. We must make that clear and distinct.

If we apply this line of thought to the finance professional, they have a lot of metrics: the balance sheet, working capital, return on working capital, and profits, etc. They have many metrics that are internally based. How can we connect that with the customer-centric view? Well, they can only be connected if there is an overall strategic objective for finance to act upon. A finance guy might look at the P&L or the balance sheet. Although she or he sees the task as making these documents things of beauty, they are actually only gathering figures. It's the same disconnect that we have at car factories. Despite what you may have heard, we don't have car factories. There is not one single car factory in the whole world. There are only assembly plants. Nothing is produced there, they just assemble a car out of parts and from sub-assemblies made elsewhere.

The same is true of the CFO or a finance organization; they don't produce numbers there. They just collect them and put them on a sheet. With that said, I also want to point out that we assign them the credit for a lot of numbers and conditions they may not actually have created – sometimes good and sometimes bad. The only thing they are doing is assembling figures and presenting them according to rules and regulations determined by others.

So, with this background, is it possible to make finance customer-centric? Yes it is. If you're looking specifically at the treasury, for instance, then you can connect it, because they are actually financing investments that should create value for the customer. But if it's only the finance department or the accounting department, where you crunch numbers and pay your suppliers, it is more difficult.

When we build a new store somewhere, there is a clear opening date from which we derive the whole plan. Everything is not financed at once, but in different stages. First, you need to buy the land, then you need to build the store, and so on and so forth. Down the road you will need to employ people. Sometimes you have to a build an access road or invest in other infrastructure. It all costs a lot of money.

If we miss out on any one piece of this, we fail and that cannot be allowed to happen. Treasury's customer-centric performance measurement must be,

"Did we bring the right amount of money at the right time, at the right cost, to be able to open the store as planned?" That is a direct connection between treasury and the customer.

While treasury is doing all this, the finance department is crunching numbers. They are helping you by creating several magic numbers, one of which is a return on capital employed. The whole organization is living and breathing this number, but the number is not important in and of itself.

What is important is what you do with that money, that huge amount of money you just earned from your new store. You will reinvest it, for instance in building your customer base, offer new products, develop existing products, etc.

This is how we should translate the profit margin we have generated into customer value. It doesn't provide any value until you actually start working with it. Just as I provide dividends in order to get more people to invest in my company, I should give something back to my customer and also put something in my pocket for a rainy day.

The finance function can be pretty siloed, or functionally oriented. If we take the finance function – perhaps including procurement – what kind of metrics, methods, and tricks do you have to help them go from a functional to a cross-functional organization?

Let's talk about the way to break down silos within a company. Often you are organized functionally, which strengthens the silos. If you examine the management team, there is likely only one person representing the customer: sales. It could be two if you have split sales and marketing, but often it's only this one person. If you have a customer contact center, the operations manager may also bring some kind of customer-centric focus.

Companies tend not to be organized from a value chain perspective. They tend to be organized in business support functions that might be the largest influencers on the management team. You have an IT department, a production department, a finance department... suddenly you don't have a company anymore. You have different companies divided along departmental lines, and everybody is a king in their own kingdom. It is no wonder these functional leaders find themselves struggling to achieve their business objectives.

Instead, companies need to start organizing themselves from a value chain perspective. Start by asking, "What do we do that creates value?" That gives you one value chain within which you have the support functions: a purchasing guy, a finance guy, a designer, and so on and so forth. I'm a proponent of matrix organizations; they work very well for me because I don't believe in hierarchies. I believe in flat organizations with the matrix axis being functionally focused and customer process-focused, or efficiency-focused, you could call it. Because you still need both. You still need to have someone who is inside-out and someone customer centric or outside-in to balance the perspectives.

I want to emphasize that customer-centricity does not mean that the customer is always right, or knows it all, creating the need to follow them to 100 percent. But we need to think outside of the silos. We can improve continuously every day, but we should talk to each other more and differently. We see opportunities, and instead of joining forces we often blame each other, which helps no one.

How shall the CEO of a company with a matrix organization pull it all together so he or she can manage it? Shall there be two separate management teams: one made up of business managers and one representing the internal support functions?

No, I don't think so. Why would I need a corporate support function on my management team? You still have support functions involved, but if you look at any management team agenda today, it starts with finance. It's always, "Give us the latest finance update." But why? Why don't we start with the latest updates regarding customers? How happy are they? How many did we win? How many did we lose? What does it all cost us? Then, afterward, finance can provide information on what the return on capital employed is or what the profits are. That's fine, but we could benefit from changing our focus and priorities.

Let's consider for a moment an example of a company who had 80 percent happy customers and 20 percent unhappy ones. Bad results come from unhappy customers. I knew of a company that won a distinguished survey on customer satisfaction. In that industry, the survey was highly regarded. This company actually managed to get 82 percent happy customers and came out as the winner.

So they achieved 82 percent customer satisfaction and the company communicated, "Look! We are best in class at 82 percent. We won! We are the best performers! There is cake in the kitchen for everyone to celebrate."

By my way of thinking, which is, of course, more customer-centric, why would I celebrate when 18 percent of my customers are dissatisfied? That is a shame! That is naïve. That is foolish. That is dangerous. That is not respecting my customers. Eighteen percent of my customer base is not happy, but I celebrate with cake. The focus should be on achieving a 100 percent customer approval rate.

It is true that 100 percent might be an overly ambitious benchmark, but I would not be satisfied with 82 percent. If it were 97 percent, then that's fine. Have cake. If I went somewhere to buy a product as an individual consumer, I would not pick the one with an 18 percent dissatisfaction rate. Unfortunately, in this particular industry it happened to be the norm. Among the blind, the one-eyed man is king, and this company had one eye. They may have been better than the rest, but if you ask me that is not a cause for celebration.

When I actually looked into the figures – this is the interesting part – I found other results. I wondered how they had performed over time. They started using the customer satisfaction measurement in 2011 with an initial measurement of 85.5 percent happy customers. From the time the measurement started they had actually lost three and a half points. Why would anyone have a cake to celebrate that?

So were they celebrating because their competition performed worse? No, they didn't. They were so internally focused that their own top rating blinded them to the larger trend – one that was absolutely having a negative effect on customers. I'm just saying if you win with 82 percent it means the other companies had a continuously bad rating too. It turned out that this company went from being top of the class with 85.5 percent in 2011, to being top of the class at 82 percent a few years later. The industry was clearly in decline and still the company didn't take the time to look at the whole statistic. They just took one number that seemed like good news and focused on that. I would have said to their CEO, "Shame on you! You should not celebrate because you have 18 percent dissatisfied customers. Secondly, you have just seen the second largest drop in satisfaction since the measurement was started. That is no reason to celebrate."

It doesn't seem like the celebration was a good message to the rest of the organization. But… and there is always a "but…" in fact they did have a reason to celebrate. In the middle of the period, somewhere in 2013, they had hit an all-time low of 79 percent satisfaction. At the same time, they started investing in a change management program within the company. They changed everything. Normally when you do that, your customer feels it and tend to rate you lower. But from the point where they started making changes, they actually grew 3 percent from their all-time low. They would have been better off positioning the celebration differently, putting the customer truly in the center by saying, "We've come far but we still have lots of potential ahead of us. Let's roll up our sleeves and remain the industry leader by an even wider margin." The 3 percent gain should have celebrated and not the 82 percent.

Earlier I gave the example of an HR person saying, "We need to hire five new full-time staff and provide this kind of training – the cost of which needs to be added to my budget." I can think of a similar example where the legal department said, "We need more legal advisers." So I said, "Okay. Why do you want those legal advisers? What are they going to add to what we are currently doing?" And they couldn't tell me. So I pressed further, "We already have so many advisers. Are you looking for specific ones who can handle real estate, or bank issues, or land negotiations? What do you need? What are you trying to accomplish? You can't just say, 'I want to hire more legal advisers.'"

I wanted them to rethink what they had asked for and connect their request to what we could accomplish for customers. If the strategy was to acquire more land to be able to build a new shopping center, then okay, then I need them because that is part of a growth strategy. They could have connected the legal advisers to that, but what was their rationale? Did they believe they had too much to do? Yes! First of all, they said they had a lot to do. And I said, "Sometimes it's not about what you're doing. It's how you're doing it." I wanted them to take a deep look at their team and find ways to some continuous improvements in their existing processes and resource allocation. We can never forget that every person which is hired, even if doing so makes things easier for current staff, is an additional cost for the customer.

Conclusion

Peter puts finance into the context of value creation for the customer. He also provides examples of how that can be done and highlights the fact that current finance practices, to a large degree, are non-value added for the customer, and non-value-added activities shall be eliminated. Finance should therefore engage with other constituents to provide a new sort of value. Expanding out of the silo is therefore a way to remain relevant.

One of the reasons companies tend to be functionally siloed is because organizational structure reinforces this through departments and hierarchy. Without taking a different approach to management and organization, companies may be at risk of having much of their work carried out far from those who have a clear understanding of the customer perspective, sometimes even taking customer value contribution out of the equation altogether. When everyone is customer-focused, silos will disappear automatically.

Peter addresses the importance of process flows in the context of how to organize the management team. He favors matrix organizations and questions if management support (that is, non-customer-focused) units shall participate at all. This means only value-added functions/processes shall govern the company. To further explore that case, he distinguishes between the inside-out and outside-in perspectives. According to Peter, you can have cake (or other positive incentives) if you organize the process with the benefits of the customer in mind. You cannot have cake if the company falls into internally-driven habits and develops silos.

Peter indirectly points to the need for everyone in the supply chain to innovate in parallel when he says that when you have a customer perspective, you will also force suppliers and distributors to share it. When you focus on the customers, you must constantly adapt to their changing needs and create new offerings to stay competitive. This forces a culture of innovation throughout the company and into the supply chain.

Key Take-Aways

- Investments such as talent and process improvements are only worthwhile if they create benefits for customers. Otherwise, the time required to design and make these changes is more likely to distract or obscure actual customer wants and needs.
- When an organization, and the functions it is comprised of, are customer-centric, they all share a common point of view rather than a series of siloed perspectives.
- Everyone at the C-level in a company should view their goals and work as customer-centric and drive these values down into the organization.
- Every measurement must be discussed in terms of how it translates to the customer experience. We must make that connection clear and distinct.
- The matrix organization is superior at combining customer focus (outside-in) with a functional focus (inside-out).
- Don't confuse customer-centric with 'the customer is always right'.
- The finance function doesn't actually produce anything; it crunches numbers. Define what customer value finance *does* create to maintain the right focus.

Peter Huber has a long and successful background in procurement and supply chain management. He recently held a position within IKANO S.A as Group Process Manager. Peter has 15 years of extensive experience from working with supply chain management in various global companies, including Metso and IKEA. IKANO is involved in insurance, real estate, and banking and also owns all of the IKEA stores in Southeast Asia. In 2017, Peter returned to IKEA.

11

Building Competitive Advantage by Connecting the Physical and Financial Chains: A Study of UPS and DHL

Magnus Lind and Kelly Barner

Summary

UPS and Deutsche Post's DHL are renowned as two of the world's largest couriers/small parcel carriers. To some of their customers, however, this is no longer the most valuable service they provide.

Over the past few years, both companies have developed financial supply chain products. Each product leverages different parts of working capital management. There are products that manage their clients' receivables, others that manage payables, and yet others that manage the actual stock. Of the three, services to address payables and receivables were already far more accessible than stock (or inventory) financing. Inventory was an area where few had come up with a serious and robust answer to the market's needs. Creating inventory financing solutions is a challenge for a host of reasons (including regulatory and tax complexities) and therefore it takes quite a long time to develop. UPS and DHL invested in financial services to differentiate themselves, to drive value for their clients, to clarify their value proposition, and to move the business development conversation away from trucks and pallets and basic material handling logistics.

By financing client inventory, UPS and DHL simultaneously take goods and transit financing off their customers' balance sheets and increase the chosen courier's 'stickiness' as a brand. Investing in the financial supply chain is

M. Lind
Skanor Group Ltd, London, UK

K. Barner
Buyers Meeting Point, Shrewsbury, MA, USA

© The Author(s) 2018
M. Lind, K. Barner, *Finance Unleashed*, DOI 10.1007/978-3-319-66370-8_11

an effective move to maintain and increase market share, not just against the other major players in the logistics space, but also when UPS and DHL find themselves in competition with small, localized players that have built enough loyalty in a contained market to cut into the larger players' margins. Introducing financial components to their service agreements changes client relationships, making UPS and DHL business-critical partners to their customers through finance. Rather than being known for their courier services, a largely commoditized offering, they can become strategic partners climbing the value chain in the eyes of their customers.

What this case presents is an example of the blurred line between what a bank offers to the market and what the non-financial industry can offer. UPS and DHL have not become funders or banks, but rather something entirely new – providers of total infrastructure for end-to-end supply chain management.

Differentiation in a Red Ocean Market

In North America, UPS has invested in the development of extended financial solutions through their UPS Capital division since 1998.[1] DHL is in the process of introducing their finance offering in Europe. This chapter presents an example of how CFOs in the logistics industry have innovated and diversified both their revenue streams and the value proposition of their business model. By doing so, they increase the buying power of their customers' wallets and reinforce their loyalty through the creation of additional value.

Both UPS's and DHL's physical supply chain services play in a competitive market that, in many cases, nears commoditization. The market has been optimized to the point that it has created a cutthroat "red ocean market," as defined by W. Chan Kim and Renée Mauborgne, the creators of Blue Ocean Strategy. "They observed that companies tend to engage in head-to-head competition in search of sustained profitable growth. Yet in today's overcrowded industries competing head-on results in nothing but a bloody red ocean of rivals fighting over a shrinking profit pool. Lasting success increasingly comes, not from battling competitors, but from creating blue oceans of untapped new market spaces ripe for growth."[2]

Although UPS and DHL are major players in the global logistics space, they must still compete with smaller players on a regular basis. These micro-competitors or 'local heroes' can often operate with a lower cost base and are more targeted to a specific community or geographical area. In these cases, it can be difficult for UPS and DHL to maintain sufficient profit margins. If they can leverage the financial supply chain to differentiate their solution and make customer relationships more 'sticky', then they have an opportunity to increase profitability by protecting their margins while delivering something of value in return. This is precisely the kind of untapped value creation Kim and Mauborgne refer to in Blue Ocean Strategy. Continuing to battle competitors would likely lead to a race to the bottom on pricing. Creating a financial services offering is more complex and requires more investment, but it is a more sustainable way to protect – and even grow – market share.

Financial Services Built to Spec

UPS and DHL chose to develop their own solutions, even though they have been offered the opportunity to enter into relationships for third-party factoring by major clients in the past. This would have ended up being quite expensive – so expensive that it could not be justified as the basis for a sustainable business model. They took control and developed their own products in such a way that allows them to approach a client and offer favorable services at attractive prices. Over time, and thanks in large part to their size, UPS and DHL have been able to negotiate competitive rates with the banks and then use them to finance their customers' supply chains.

Both companies made significant investments in inventory management as a way of improving product attractiveness and differentiating themselves in the face of stiff pricing competition. Since inventory moves within each company's existing logistics network, they have sufficient control and visibility to provide security for the financing and manage their own risk (and the banks') exposure.

With these new financial products, customers immediately experience significant measurable value. Some clients may initially have been skeptical about the new approach to inventory financing. They may have wanted to address their receivables and payables first, waiting to look at inventory at a later point. If companies are to rely on non-financial suppliers (such as UPS or DHL) to act as intermediaries to the banks, they will need to understand the implications for bank relationships and the availability of funding in times of financial stress. These deepened customer relationships bring many benefits, but also heightened responsibilities for UPS and DHL. Being a business-critical supplier that may be difficult, risky, and expensive to replace is a very different ballgame than being a provider of a commodity service that is here today and gone tomorrow.

Growing Offerings Without Losing Focus

When non-financial companies decide to add financial components to their services, they must understand how it will affect the role and operation of their core offerings. Like any other company considering this approach, UPS and DHL do not want to become banks. This is too big a diversion and it comes with the potential risk of allowing financial industry regulations and compliance requirements to restrict their core business. Instead, they want to carve out a position as the middleman (or partner) with banks and fintech companies on behalf of their customers. They will, for instance, finance their customers' receivables by setting up an alternate third-party structure that purchases the receivables being funded by a major bank. The funding should be non-recourse other than from an operational point of view. For example, if there is a problem with a product financed through such a program, then there is the form of recourse, but from a financial credit point of view the arrangement is non-recourse.

Non-financial companies don't usually want to be put in a position where they are competing directly with banks and other traditional financial institutions. Geographically driven regulations provide the answer to this. Banks are prevented from offering 'global' services by new financial regulations that force them to regionalize. UPS and DHL, however, can partner with several banks to offer extensive coverage to each customer (regardless of location) and become a sort of a distributor of the banks' services. The banks are thus provided with the opportunity to reach out to the whole supply chain of UPS's and DHL's customers.

DHL stressed their desire to "focus on core competencies in mail and global logistics businesses" when they sold Postbank in 2009.[3] The CEO was adamant that while DHL may walk a fine line, they will not get too close to the banking area again; however, they opened up for a continued partnership with Postbank.

This is an important point for any CFO intending to add innovative financial solutions to their client offerings. The financial product should not become the key product. Instead, it should facilitate and provide value to complement the base offering. All financial risks have to be outsourced to the banks or other third parties and the organization should remain focused on their core service (unless they *want* to be a bank).

The Value of the Whole Is More Than the Sum of Its Many Parts

When financial and non-financial companies integrate their services, the party that owns the customer relationship in the physical supply chain will likely become the face of the financial supply chain as well. With these kinds of solutions, the financial supply chain is integrated in the same way as the physical chain and covers a broader service scope than what the banks currently do. The banks will likely continue to work gradually with a smaller number of non-financial companies, and only with large ones such as UPS and DHL. The banks may use them to reach the rest of the corporate market.

The addition of fintech solutions such as supplier portals and invoice management tools allows UPS and DHL to offer higher-level automation and services breadth than the banks. Customers get access to an infrastructure that integrates the management of products and cash flow. They receive funding, invoice and payables management, and logistics services from one supplier on a global basis. The clients gain full visibility into their transactions all the way through the process on one combined technical platform branded UPS or DHL.

Given the fact that two major players have already taken the step of integrating financial services into their offering, it is likely that competition will drive them to incorporate more capabilities in the future. Such expansion options include payment functionality, credit insurance, and credit management offered through similar integrations with payment providers and major credit insurers.

Reaching a Natural State of Alignment

Which part of the business will be the core going forward, logistics or financing? Let's answer that question by regarding it from another perspective: why do we separate the flow of cash, or real money, from the flow of products and services? Doing so is unnatural given the fact that no products or services can be delivered without the exchange of funds in return. The financial and physical supply chains are naturally linked. Perhaps the division of suppliers in the financial and physical chains is not a normal state, but rather a result of how banks had to operate before the introduction of the Internet. The Internet has changed the concept of trust, an element that is paramount for the financial industry, and which improves transparency for the distribution of capital and financial risk in the supply chain. CFOs and CEOs understand how factors such as trust and transparency have the power to change (and perhaps even disrupt) whole industries. This is why the new role of the CFO contains a wider scope of working capital effectiveness covering the whole supply chain and why innovation will be a core theme going forward for all finance executives.

The CFOs at DHL and UPS have managed to enhance their client offering, increase their margins, and strengthen their company's competitiveness.

When clients join them to discuss contract renewals, the initial focus is likely to be aggressive price cutting based on the strength of existing alternatives for logistics, courier services, and small parcel delivery. When the financial infrastructure piece is added, however, and the customer understands what it means for their business, the discussion changes completely. All of a sudden, the costs clients were looking to reduce on warehousing and transport seem unimportant, despite the fact that this is where UPS and DHL have earned their household names. The leverage balance changes completely at that point; all of a sudden, the integrated offering becomes much 'stickier' and the relationship becomes more advantageous for all parties.

Small logistics players and local companies will have a big problem competing in this new landscape. Offering financial services is something that they cannot do, but that does not mean that the competitive pressure to innovate will subside. As DHL and UPS broaden their value proposition, they will encounter new competitors and innovate similarly novel ways to add to their logistics and finance offerings. As the financial and physical supply chains integrate further, many of the current dis-intermediators may disappear and more 'global' solutions will become the norm.

Conclusion

In this example, the finance function has taken charge of customer innovation and engaged all stakeholders in the company. The UPS/DHL case is a good example of how the CFO can take a role as a disruptive business driver. The CFO responded to competitive pressures, not only through cost cutting, but also through the creation of new revenue streams.

UPS and DHL have proven that the CFO can provide business value and disrupt a whole industry by pushing it from a low-profitability, competitive market to a so-called 'blue ocean' market. They found a need their customers didn't yet recognize and filled it effectively. This is rare; usually innovators allow their customer to specify improvements and adjust or build the offering out of those specifications. The UPS and DHL innovation takes this a step further by offering something the customer needed without knowing it, as in this famous quote commonly attributed to Henry Ford: "If I'd asked the customers what they wanted, they'd have asked for faster horses."[4]

UPS and DHL assist finance and risk manage supply chains from their dominating role in logistics. The effect from their customers' point of view is that they connect the financial and physical supply chains and distribute capital more optimally. Rather than engaging in a race to the bottom on margins, they decided to add something to their product portfolio that no one else could – financing. This has made them 'stickier' with current customers and helped them win new customers. UPS and DHL did this by partnering with fintech vendors, banks, credit insurers, and other financial institutions. UPS and DHL effectively packaged the capabilities of these products to provide a less fragmented and more customer-adapted solution.

Key Take-Aways

- When faced with rising competition and falling profit margins, broadening the customer value proposition is an alternative to placing all faith in downward pressure on operational costs.
- Despite the positive reactions to this new financing program, leadership teams must be certain that they want it to become a competitive differentiator for their core business, instead of a new core offering.
- When a non-financial company adds financial components to its offerings, it must act carefully to avoid becoming a victim of financial regulation and not risk being categorized as a bank. The physical service or product should remain the core.
- The CFO is in a position to drive the creation of stickier, healthier, and more profitable client relations.
- The unnatural divide between the financial and the physical supply chains can be expected to decrease as the chains become more integrated.

Notes

1. "UPS Capital: Company History," Accessed July 1, 2017, https://upscapital.com/about-us/company-history/.
2. "What is Blue Ocean Strategy?" Accessed July 1, 2017, https://www.blue-oceanstrategy.com/what-is-blue-ocean-strategy/.
3. DHL Global, *Deutsche Post DHL Completes Postbank Transaction*, February 28, 2012, http://www.dhl.com/en/press/releases/releases_2012/group/022812.html.
4. Patrick Vlaskovits, "Henry Ford, Innovation, and That 'Faster Horse' Quote," *Harvard Business Review*, August 29, 2017, https://hbr.org/2011/08/henry-ford-never-said-the-fast.

12

Back to the Future

Charles Bean

Summary

Sir Charles (Charlie) Bean puts the financial supply chain into a historical perspective by presenting parallels and similarities from his background as a central bank governor and economist. Globalization is nothing new; the need to fund and financially risk manage global supply chains has been around for hundreds of years. With his deep knowledge of trade and policy making, however, he points at trends and previous solutions that can provide the historical answers to our current questions.

Interview with Sir Charles (Charlie) Bean conducted September 16, 2016

Amongst other things, this book focusses on an apparent convergence of the financial and physical supply chains. For instance, there is the example in Chapter 11 of UPS and DHL who manage complex logistics for their clients, but have added a finance component, enabling their clients to finance payables, receivables, and inventory.

Funnily enough, this is quite like what the Bank of England did way back in the nineteenth and twentieth centuries. If a manufacturer or merchant had an agreement to deliver goods for which he could not expect to be paid immediately – say, because of the time needed to ship them around the world – he could nevertheless get paid by the Bank straight away. There would be a so-called 'Bill of Exchange' or a promise to pay from the buyer to the producer. The producer could take that to the Bank of England and say, "Here, I've got this promise that

Charles Bean
London School of Economics, London, UK

© The Author(s) 2018
M. Lind, K. Barner, *Finance Unleashed*, DOI 10.1007/978-3-319-66370-8_12

I'm going to get this money in three months' time. Will you give me some money now?" The Bank of England would charge a small fee – a discount, to be technical – and that would enable the merchant to get their money immediately. Eventually, the money would be paid to the Bank of England by the person buying the goods rather than by the manufacturer or merchant.

This was effectively an early version of collateralized lending: merchants had collateral in the form of the promise that they could borrow against. Other commercial banks also carried out this sort of activity.

If you go back to the late nineteenth century and the Edwardian era, before the outbreak of the First World War, the international economy was surprisingly highly integrated. Much of this trade took place within the British Empire, while much of the finance underpinning it was through bills of exchange drawn in London. The empire helped make this system viable because it provided a common legal framework and other necessary common procedures. Of course, the bank had to be confident that the end-buyer was going to honor his commitment to buy the goods and pay up. Without that trust, the collateral of the promise to pay would hold little value.

The Bank of England was actually founded in 1694 to help the sovereign finance his foreign wars – indeed, in the Bank's founding charter there are all sorts of things about beating the French! The Bank's mission has obviously changed since then, yet through the eighteenth and into the early nineteenth centuries, the Bank of England was in many ways like any other bank. Because it was regarded as a particularly safe bank and was operated on quite conservative principles, over time it came to serve as a banker to other banks. So it wasn't actually *created* as the central bank we now know it as. Over time it gradually acquired the functions that we now associate with central banks and, in particular, the role of being a lender of last resort to private banks that get into difficulties. This was something that developed further through the twentieth century as well.

In fact, the Bank was nationalized only fairly recently – after the war in 1946. Prior to that it was basically a private bank, and if you look at UK bank notes, it still says that it is the "Governor and Company of the Bank of England" who will honor the promise to turn the note into gold, and it is still the case that the directors are listed at Companies House (where all commercial companies are listed in the UK). But since nationalization, Her Majesty's Treasury has owned all the shares, whereas previously they were owned by financial institutions.

From the outset, then, the Bank was endowed with particular tasks and responsibilities. But in many ways, it did act like a regular bank. It took deposits and it lent both to the government and to private individuals and businesses. Then, over time, it mutated into the role of being a lender to banks and stopped being a general lender to businesses.

So, if we return to the present, technological and regulatory developments pose significant challenges to the conventional banking model. In part, this is because the past profitability of banks was based on the idea of having a highly levered balance sheet. Banks had relatively small amounts of equity capital, took in short-term deposits or possibly debt raised on the capital market, and then lent it out long term to individuals and companies who wanted to buy homes or capital assets. The business model is thus based on the idea that depositors can withdraw their money on demand, but not everybody is likely to come and withdraw it all at once.

That's fine in normal circumstances. But a problem arises when it turns out that a bank has a lot of loans that have gone bad or that its lending has been too concentrated in particular areas. For instance, in the mid-nineteenth century, a lot of loans were granted to railway companies and when it was clear that the banks had overextended themselves, a banking crisis followed. Similarly, the recent financial crisis was created through excessive lending to subprime households who, it subsequently transpired, were unlikely to be able to pay those mortgages back. If depositors learn that their bank has made a lot of bad loans, they are likely to rush to withdraw their deposits in case the bank runs out of money, leading to a bank run. One of the roles of central banks is to act as a *lender of last resort* to the banks when too many of their depositors want to withdraw their money at once.

One consequence of the recent financial crisis is that regulators realized banks had been operating with far too little equity to absorb potential losses. Moreover, debt holders also generally assumed that they would always be repaid and so did not penalize risky lending by the bank's management. Post-crisis, we have therefore seen significant increases in the capital banks are required to hold relative to their assets. That has encouraged banks to shrink their balance sheets, at least in the first instance. Moreover, the reduction in the implicit subsidy offered by the prospect of state support if a bank gets into difficulties has rendered the conventional bank business model less profitable than it was. There is now a real challenge for banks as to how they can add sufficient value in intermediating funds from depositors through to borrowers to be profitable.

At the same time, advances in information technology make it easier for other intermediaries to step in and play the role that banks have traditionally done. A key thing that a bank is supposed to do is to concentrate deposits from depositors and then decide who is a good firm or household to lend to. The bank sets appropriate interest charges to reflect the risks of lending in each case. It makes sense, in principle, just to have one agent doing that rather than all of the individual depositors, so banks have consistently played this key screening role. However, with the advances in information technology, it's potentially much easier for information about companies to be shared and to emerge from a range of people. Peer-to-peer lending is based on the idea that you don't need to rely on a single intermediary who's doing due diligence on a borrower, but you can instead rely on the wisdom and knowledge of crowds about the potential creditworthiness of a borrower or the value of their ideas.

This takes us into the interesting area of how to measure credit risk. The current regulatory framework (the Basel Accord) was originally introduced in the 1980s and was based on the premise that the evaluation of credit risks could be based on set formulas rather than relying on human intervention and judgment. It thus facilitated the movement from 'relationship-based banking' to 'arm's-length banking' and laid the foundation for the growth of rating agencies able to provide the ratings necessary for the calculations. With time, that led to more and more complex formulas until it finally became impossible to understand what the true credit risks actually were.

Pre-crisis there was a lot of reliance on a sort of tick-box mentality: credit scores and the like. In the run-up to the crisis, bankers would claim "We know our balance sheets have been exploding and we may be doing a lot of lending, but we're much better at managing risk now." They would say they were more scientific about risk evaluation. But we discovered during the crisis that their risk management was not quite as good as they thought.

That partly accounts for why people are now looking at other mechanisms. But there is a risk with some of these peer-to-peer lending platforms that, in the long run, we will discover that some of what people thought was knowledge about potential borrowers wasn't really knowledge at all, but was instead gut feeling that could easily go wrong in one way or another. It wouldn't surprise me if there are scandals further down the road resulting from people who have been persuaded to put their money into particular companies based on incorrect or incomplete information of one sort or another. Yet, in principle, I'm sure there will be some models of that sort which survive, as long as they are focused on the idea of sharing information about the company from lots of different sources to help people judge whether they're a good credit or investment risk or not.

Credit scoring is definitely not a simple task, and we will have to continue to rely on sound judgment and close monitoring. Yet the banks are currently exposed to disruptive competition driven by technology and need to up their game. For instance, it is surprising that it has taken the banks as long as it has to get to a position where payments clear in the space of an hour or two at most. For small payments, it's now instantaneous, whereas previously it would take up to five days for a payment to be credited to your account. That was symptomatic of a rather sluggish embracement of what is possible with modern information technology.

Another effect of the recent crisis has been a retreat by some international banks to their home markets: the so-called 'de-globalization' of banking. A more localized banking industry means that a multinational company active in, say 20 countries, might need to have almost as many bankers, thus introducing extra costs and complexities into their operations.

However, we should also recognize that there are benefits from this. Banks typically know more about their domestic markets than they do know about foreign markets. Where banks often come unstuck is when they engage in foreign ventures that they don't properly understand. For instance, the Royal Bank of Scotland (RBS) really came unstuck because it bought the worst bits of ABN AMRO and also some toxic US mortgage-backed securities. Similarly, the undoing of some of the German Landesbanks lay in their purchases of US mortgage-backed securities that they did not properly understand. Things typically go wrong when an investor – whether it's a bank or some other financial institution – gets involved in something they don't know quite so well and treats information from the rating agencies, such as the AAA rating of mortgage-backed securities, as an inviolable guide, rather than taking it with an appropriate pinch of salt.

In principle, one response to this de-globalization of banking, where you've got multinational corporations who are operating in lots of different markets and there are lots of different elements in the supply chain, lies in creating networks of correspondent banks across jurisdictions. So although the individual banks might be domestically focused, they're in alliances with correspondent banks in other jurisdictions. Together, they can then provide joined-up services corresponding to the needs of the multinational or the supply chain businesses that operate across lots of different national boundaries.

Some argue that correspondent banking is not the way forward since the set-up is too expensive. They instead look to totally new solutions for trade finance, for instance, saying they will destroy correspondent banking in the same way that Skype destroyed cellphone roaming charges. So what I'm suggesting is just one potential solution. However it's not the only one. And with multiple possibilities, there is the question of which is most efficient. Certainly, thinking about the supply chain as a holistic entity rather than in separate bits may help point the way to exploiting synergies and utilizing collateral in new ways. If you're just dealing with one particular entity in a supply chain and you don't know very much about the other bits in the supply chain, then the value of obligations from one bit of the supply chain to another is collateral. There ought to be value to the information that is embedded throughout the supply chain if you can access it and lever off it.

Let's now turn to another event I've been involved with and might be interesting in this context, namely the review I was commissioned by the government to undertake as to whether the UK's economic statistics are still fit for purpose in the digital age. The first thing the review observed – and I'm not the first to make this observation – is that the frame of reference we use for measuring the economy typically lags a long way behind reality. At the moment, if you look at the industrial classification that is used in all countries, about half of the industries are manufacturing. Yet for the UK, manufacturing accounts for only about 10 percent of GDP. There is inadequate detail in the services sector. Instead you've just got some really broad aggregates.

This is not the first time we've faced this issue. If you go back and look at the statistical abstract for the UK at the end of the nineteenth century, it had a couple of hundred pages on agriculture and trade with the empire and just a handful of pages on industrial activity at the end. Whereas, of course, industry was the big driver of the Industrial Revolution! Now, at the close of the twentieth century, we don't have anything like as good a picture of what is going on in services as we do in manufacturing.

A lack of granularity is not the only issue. On top of that, you need to recognize that services are intrinsically harder to measure than manufacturing outputs. In the old days, when a lot of it was iron or steel, you could just almost think of weighing the output, because you had products coming out. You can count how many cars a car manufacturer produces, and so on. Services are more heterogeneous, and the nature of the price for the service is often less clear.

In particular, there are a lot of challenges associated with services provided in the digital economy, because they are supplied through unusual business models. The way the national accounts are set up presumes that the value to the consumer is basically reflected by the price paid and there is an observable price at the point where the goods change hands. But in the digital economy, the mode of payment is often different. Digital products might be quite costly to produce, but then can be replicated at virtually zero marginal cost. Producers of a digital product therefore want to get very high levels of market penetration for their particular product. Once they've got that, they can do things like selling advertising space or else information about their consumers to other parties. A lot of digital firms finance their activities not by charging for the content, which is provided at zero or minimal charge, but rather by getting lots of customers in and then charging the advertisers to use the website as a way of getting their message across.

Now the way the national accounts aggregates are defined, if you've got a digital provider who provides services at zero price and finances activities by selling advertising space, because advertising is treated as an intermediate expense, it nets out for value added in the economy as a whole, so the contribution to overall GDP is calculated as zero. Consequently, we're in a world where some of the services that are being generated just don't get picked up using conventional measurement methods.

Another feature my review discussed is the disintermediation from the market economy of some sorts of activities. GDP is not really a measure of standard of living and economists always pay lip service to that. Yet we still treat the growth of GDP as an indicative answer to the question: "Are things getting better or not?" To give you one example of how the movements in GDP might be misleading, think of booking a holiday. In the old days, you would have gone down to your High street travel agent. Then you spent an hour or two sitting with them, talking about possibilities, maybe looking at a few brochures and going home afterward. Eventually, you'd go back to the travel agent and say, "Yes, I want to go to a such and such place," and then the travel agent would go through all the business of booking with the holiday company or the airline and whatever. Then you book a hotel to stay in and you buy a guidebook and all those sorts of things.

What would you do today? You go online to do the initial research, which is all freely available. You use TripAdvisor. You decide where you want to go and then book directly with the airline. You also directly book your hotel or else use Airbnb so you're staying in somebody's home and they're essentially acting as a part-time hotelier. You use free Google Maps to get around rather than buying a guidebook. The travel agent – who previously was adding value as an intermediary – has been completely cut out of the process. Also, consider the hotelier; in principle, the rental through Airbnb might get picked up but I'll bet a lot of people who rent out their homes for the two weeks that they're away on holiday don't declare it to the tax authorities, so the activity there might not be getting properly picked up either.

Measured GDP will be adversely affected by this change in the way people are doing things, and if you're thinking about whether people are better off doing it this way than going through the travel agent, then you would say yes. We are better off because information technology has made it much easier for people to do the necessary information processing themselves. These are all the sorts of things that were not possible until the advent of fast computers and the Internet as a way of transferring information between individuals and companies.

Let's take a look at another example where measurement has become more difficult: allowing for quality improvement. We are not really just interested in the cash amount of an expenditure, but want to know how much "stuff" that expenditure buys. So we need to abstract from changes in the quantity of expenditure that result from a general rise in prices to get at the "real" change in spending. But how do statistical agencies go about measuring the general rise in prices?

What statistical agencies are trying to do is estimate what is happening to the cost of a *fixed* basket of goods. There's a long list of products which are in this representative basket and in the UK each month the statisticians and their teams go out with clipboards to supermarkets and corner shops and they note down the price of a brown loaf, a white loaf, croissants, etc. There are lots of different sorts of bread that they'll be taking the price of, and they do the same for lots of other different products. They do that every month, and as far as possible, it's a fixed basket and they go to the same outlets each month. That allows them to compare the price of a given product from one month to the next. You can weight them all together and get an average change in the price level. You can then divide money spending by this price index to get a measure of how the amount of 'stuff' ('real GDP') is moving.

But the nature of products changes and this greatly complicates the process. Croissants may not change much in quality over the years, but many tech products certainly do. Take computers, for instance. The first laptop that you could carry around cost about £4,000 and it had only 7 kilobytes of RAM. Today, a laptop costs around £600 and has several gigabytes of RAM and can do so much more than its predecessor. The price of a laptop might have come down quite a bit, but the laptop today also does vastly more than the laptop that you bought several years ago and you need to allow for that improvement in quality in compiling measures of inflation and real GDP.

Measuring quality change is very difficult. Statisticians have various methods for trying to do it and they recognize that they're all imperfect. What they do with something like a computer is they don't look at the price of the computer itself. What they try to do instead is ask what services the computer provides – computing power, for instance – and then work out what the price of a unit of computing power is. This is done using something called *hedonics*, which requires attaching a price to each of the characteristics that the product provides. These hedonic methods which look at, say, the price of a unit of RAM, are the way they do that. What you would find is that the price of a computer is actually falling *much* faster than would be shown through an approach that simply compares the cost to me of a typical laptop 20 years ago with the cost of one today.

Something like a smartphone is even more complex. It not just a better phone. It's a camera. It's a music player. It's a navigational device. It's a game console. It does all sorts of things. How you encapsulate the difference between that and a mobile phone of 15, 20 years ago in the GDP statistics is a delicate and difficult problem. Even just allowing for changes in one vintage of iPhone to the next presents a challenge!

These sorts of quality change issues are a really big deal for technology products, simply because the product changes so rapidly. In other areas of expenditure, quality change is much slower and most obviously so with food.

Moreover, quality change in existing products is not the only issue. Another challenge arises from the broadening of choice as completely new products are developed. One of the things that doesn't get picked up in the official statistical measures of inflation is the effect of this broadening in choice because they look at the evolution of the cost of a fixed basket of goods and services over time. Periodically, what's in the basket is updated, but the sheer fact that the consumer can choose from a huge range of things now whereas they had a much more restricted choice in the past, isn't captured.

The bottom line from all this is that our measures of inflation and economic activity are probably becoming increasingly less reliable guides than they once were.

Conclusion

One of the tasks of finance is to ensure liquidity, funding, and trade finance. Here Charlie describes these tasks in an economic context and explains how these practices have developed over time. Charlie starts by presenting how the Bank of England made factoring available for export and import firms through bills of exchange over a century ago. As a central banker and economist, he takes a more holistic process flow perspective than do most corporations. From Charlie's description, isolating finance seems irrelevant.

Charlie relates to the customer by considering how the financial system can support growth and by proving the need for a well-functioning and stable financial platform. He notes that one of the consequences of the financial crisis has been some de-globalization of banking (withdrawing to their home markets in order to reduce risks) while the business world has been moving in the opposite direction. That has complicated the provision of financial services to multinational companies. One solution is thorough networks of correspondent banks, although technological advances may mean other solutions are now viable.

Economic statistics, such as GDP and inflation, are key indicators for business. Charlie notes that these are becoming progressively less reliable. Aside from the fact that the services side of the economy is not accurately measured, the digital economy is leading to new business models that are not well captured in the official statistics and the disintermediation of activities out of the market economy into home production. Finally, the challenges of allowing for quality change and new products are becoming ever greater.

Key Take-Aways

- The need for standardized, robust relationships between banks and commercial entities is not new – in England in particular, they date back to the nineteenth century. At that time, however, goods moved far more slowly than funds – at least when they were transferred in person – and it was the banks that provided valuable financial services to individuals and businesses.

- The Bank of England discounted bills of exchange in the nineteenth century to finance international supply chains.
- The Bank of England, nationalized in 1946 and previously owned by financial institutions, was originally a stable private bank gradually operating more and more as the central bank we know today.
- If you take away the development that technology now provides, the basics of banking remain the same as in the past. Standardization of legal contracts and financial products remain just as important for enabling global trade and growth.
- The current peer-to-peer (P2P) lending and financial practices are actually nothing new and may create financial instability and unknown risks. In the past, we've seen unorthodox evaluations of credit risk lead to situations of financial stress.
- In the aftermath of the 2007 financial crisis, we learned that the banks were not as good at assessing and managing risk as they had thought – a disconnect that was seen in banks' dangerously low levels of equity capital. They had an overreliance on algorithms and regulation and often applied too little common sense.
- We base many of our forecasts and business plans on economic data, such as GDP and inflation. What many of us don't consider is how these data are gathered and how the transformation from a manufacturing economy to a service – and increasingly a digital – economy has affected GDP and inflation. The new ways of calculating GDP and inflation for service economies (v. manufacturing) will likely change the magnitude of these figures.

Sir Charles Bean is Professor of Economics at the London School of Economics (LSE). From 2000 to 2014, he served at the Bank of England as, successively, Executive Director and Chief Economist, and then Deputy Governor for Monetary Policy, serving on both the Monetary Policy and Financial Policy Committees. He also represented the Bank in international fora, such as the G7 and G20. Before joining the Bank, he was a member of the faculty at LSE and he has also worked at HM Treasury. He has served as Managing Editor of the *Review of Economic Studies*, was President of the Royal Economic Society from 2013 to 2015, and is Chairman of the Centre for Economic Policy Research. He was knighted in 2014 for services to monetary policy and central banking and recently undertook a review of the quality, delivery, and governance of UK economic statistics for the UK government. He holds a PhD from MIT.

13

The Whole Chain or Separate Links?

Gary Slawther

Summary

One of the greatest risks to the performance of a company is their inability to move beyond functional silos. This is seen in the tendency to 'throw' transactions over the wall from one function to another as well as in the individually set – and often contradictory – objectives that the functions are simultaneously working toward. Ironically, the same challenge often exists within the supply chain as a whole. Whether it is companies or banks, entities would benefit from trying to understand the inner workings of the entire chain from end to end rather than approaching each link individually. Gary is an advocate of cooperating financially over the supply chain and this effort starts with the linking of stakeholders internally.

Interview with Gary Slawther conducted August 2, 2016

One of the challenges I face is an organizational issue caused by how we operate as a business. It may not be intentional, but it often works out this way. We all tend to work in silos. We each sit with a narrow, self-built wall around us that defines what WE do and also what THEY do. A piece of paper miraculously comes from the other side of the wall to me. I do something with it and then I throw it over another side of the wall. It can be an uphill struggle to break down that mode of operation.

It is the same when you look outside of the company at how we cooperate with our suppliers and customers. I believe we would benefit from breaking down

G. Slawther
OCTAL, Raysut, Oman

© The Author(s) 2018
M. Lind, K. Barner, *Finance Unleashed*, DOI 10.1007/978-3-319-66370-8_13

those walls and barriers and making sure the whole operation is seen by those who are in it as part of one cohesive chain rather than as separate links. I think we're moving towards regarding the supply chain as a connected multi-party supply transaction which goes from the purchase of raw materials to delivery of the final product to the end-customer. When we see it as one single, extended transaction, we avoid managing it as a series of unrelated events and instead see it as individual occurrences in the lifespan of one transaction.

We should always keep the end-customer in mind when we examine all parts of the supply chain. This provides the company with a single mindset and target. It also becomes much easier to manage the company in pursuit of common goals with each and every function and the participating suppliers and distributors having their own responsibilities.

So, how am I at this end of the supply chain able to satisfy a customer at the other end of the supply chain? Well, you're satisfying them in three ways. The first is by giving them the best price for a specific value, of course. Second is to make sure the right thing is delivered to the right place at the right time. As an aside, when I was in logistics it became apparent to me that anyone can drive a truck, yet getting the right thing to the right place at the right time has massive benefits to the entire economy. As grandiose as that may sound, when you take the waste of excessive inventory and tied-up cash out of the supply chain, you save everyone a lot of time and a lot of money.

The third way to satisfy customers is by providing efficient quality: by handling the resupply and reworking of goods right the first time. Make sure everyone who sits in the quality department realizes the impact their actions have on the supply chain. If everyone is able to see themselves as being part of one long transaction instead of only a link in the chain, they might approach their work a little bit differently. This change in perspective would allow us to structure things in another way from both the physical and financial sides of the chain.

How can you start to effect this change? Do we start with how we measure performance or do we start with how we set goals? I've hinted very much at the answer – I believe it is in the way we set goals. In essence, each of the processes along the line has been individually designed. The inbound supply chain has its own design and objectives, for instance. You need to connect those objectives in any way, shape, or form to the other people and objectives along the supply chain.

Let me explain how individual, unaligned objective setting can have a negative impact.

A sales team is told, "You have to sell at a price point better than the market price, achieving at least $15 above market on this sale." That's their sole objective. The next thing that happens is that the salespeople can sell maybe 25,000 or 30,000 tons of product per month at that required price. Anything more and the marginal revenue starts to drop and you're not hitting your $15 goal so they stop selling once they reach 30,000 tons.

A procurement department is charged with buying at the best price possible and we view the best price possible as being $10 a ton less than market index. That is their objective. They work hard to comply with that objective. The easy way for a procurement person to get their costs as low as possible is to buy as much as possible from one supplier. You're allowed to volume discount so you buy 50,000 tons a month. That's great! So after six months, and with 20,000 tons of inventory on hand, the CEO asks, "What are we doing with all this inventory? We have to sweep it all through. We just have to get rid of it." So we flush all the inventory through at a great loss because usually this happens at about the worst time in the market. So we sell it all, and lo and behold, we lose money. But everyone has done their job.

They've all done their work very professionally, with a great deal of effort, and according to expectations.

This tells us that companies often have too many targets and objectives and goals set on individual and group levels. How can we understand how all these goals interact and what the company as a one whole entity is driving at?

Should we instead have only a handful of (say between three and six) corporate goals that everyone is measured on at each point in time? The whole company will work toward the same goals and everyone will contribute through their respective responsibilities. When the first goals are met, you set the next ones. It would be more of an entrepreneurial modus operandi. I believe that this is perhaps a better structure, and I would add that you must have good leaders on the ground guiding and supporting the teams to keep them motivated and productive. We established five overall targets when we were put in charge of an exercise to boost EBITDA year over year and we had a number of meetings to split the business into seven cost centers. We had a series of calls with all of them and it went very well. One thing I noticed after a while was that some key themes started to emerge around the risks that might prevent us from excelling as an organization. It all boiled down to five key risks.

I keep the five key risks written up on the board next to my desk.

Number one is *people*. We must have the right people who know what they are doing, who are properly instructed, properly incentivized, and who have non-conflicting targets.

Quality is the next risk. We must get the quality right, act fast internally, and reject scrap goods before they are able to reach our customers.

Next is *waste*. When we manufacture something, we must make the very most of the materials we use and minimize waste. This includes minimizing waste in the financial supply chain, of course.

Fourth is *customer service*. Everything we do has to be geared toward customer service and product satisfaction. We have experienced what it is like when the logistics manager is solely driven by the cheapest *freight rate* (the fifth risk), which is a huge cost for us. Only focusing on freight rates, for example, would sometimes mean the customers have to wait another four weeks for delivery. We must trust our people to be able to juggle contradictory factors and make sure the customers are satisfied because everyone understands that is what counts.

When we push this holistic goal setting further, we can detect the opportunity of streamlined trade finance, which is a view of the supply chain as one transaction instead of as separate links. I certainly believe we should view the whole chain as one entity. In fact, supply chains rarely fail, but when they do it is often due to insufficient liquidity somewhere in the chain. In principle, every part of the chain is dependent on the others. Each party is incentivized to avoid failures wherever they occur. The corporate sector takes a holistic view of the chain and shares the need for it to be robust, meaning that corporates take a chain-wide perspective. Many banks, on the other hand, are still focused on each separate link in the chain, something they have a strong self-interest in because it allows them to cherry-pick their credit exposure and engagements.

The implication of this single link point of view is that trade finance has too many intermediaries today. This often creates an unnecessary level of complexity that can lead to additional costs, longer lead times, and the inefficient 'locking-in' of capital. The lack of transparency means that it can be nearly impossible to see where capital is stuck and what is creating the slippage and waste.

In reality, the chain includes lots of risks as well as credits that could be better served if only we had a greater degree of visibility. Current trade finance processes are often creating bottlenecks and needless cost. Contemporary business demands that we eliminate them. Some form of harmonization needs to be achieved through the development of a better, more automated financial infrastructure.

The reason the system looks this way is that current trade finance relies on the correspondent banking model that is inefficient, costly, and exacerbates lead times and complexity. Since we can reasonably expect that international trade will continue to increase, driven by globalization and eCommerce, this roadblock cannot be allowed to persist for long.

I have the following hypothesis: trade finance is currently very fragmented. It separates the financing, payment, risk, and credit management that exist between each participant (or link) in the supply chain. Financial solutions tend to evaluate each link separately instead of in the context of the end-to-end chain. This can severely hamper trade, leading to a number of solutions which must be evaluated for their ability to streamline this process. There is currently a trend towards transforming invoices to bills of exchange which can be used as financing vehicles. We would expect this to mean fewer transactions, more standardization, and harmonization. We also anticipate increased demand for more holistic, customer-centric services that manage the whole trade cycle from a chain perspective.

A corporation's risk does not only lay within its own remittances. It includes the whole supply and demand chain. The most important solutions would therefore be to achieve improved transparency, answering questions such as, "Where is the working capital stuck?", "Where does it cost most?" and, "What is our net foreign exchange exposure in the chain?"

What do we risk if we can't transition to a full-chain perspective and instead remain stuck in financing and managing risk in each separate link? The risk the financial supply chain presents to physical supply chains is in preventing a greater degree of automation and transparency required for improvement. Without drastic improvements, there is a strong likelihood that trade finance in its current form will simply be bypassed as an obstacle to economic growth and wealth creation. The need for new trade finance products is undoubtedly already here.

The corporate sector is critically dependent on well-functioning and reliable trade finance solutions that can provide modern, relevant functionality in a cost-efficient way. Low-friction onboarding of these solutions will be one of the most important competitive factors, for instance, of fintech vendors.

My hypothesis is that new trade finance instruments are required and there are opportunities to exploit the current fintech developments through distributed technical models and more. We can also assume that the corporate sector might take on some of the role currently played by banks, ensuring between them that supply chains are sufficiently funded much more efficiently than they are today. The corporate sector's reliance on current trade finance practices may have created a dependence that will serve as an inhibitor to increased competitiveness.

Conclusion

As a CFO, Gary Slawther is geared toward revenue. He argues that any company's customers are looking for something relatively straightforward: desired products or services delivered as ordered and on time. Yet when you look at the myriad of functional objectives and stakeholders in a company, not everyone seems to align with what the customer wants.

Compound the effect of intra-company silos by combining all of the functions in all of the companies from raw materials to the final product delivery in the supply chain. The resulting waste and inefficiency can be staggering. Without increased automation and transparency of the financial chain, there is a strong likelihood that trade finance in its current form will simply be bypassed as an obstacle to economic growth and wealth creation.

The problem with current trade finance practices and services is that they chop up the supply chain into links that are evaluated separately rather than as part of a chain. This increases costs and lead times and reduces transparency. When the physical supply chain develops further, the current financial supply chain can provide unnecessary obstacles and friction. We can therefore anticipate that novel trade finance solutions will be developed to support the corporate sector and improve their customer offerings.

Key Take-Aways

- Finance is a function that is often siloed; we should aim at breaking down those walls.
- We should evaluate having only a few (between three and six) overarching corporate goals at any point in time that everyone is measured on. These goals can change once they are fulfilled.
- Having too many metrics and objectives in an organization allows for dissimilar goals and misalignment with customer needs – ultimately sacrificing the potential for competitive advantage.
- The financial supply chain is currently so inefficient that it may hinder the development of the physical supply chain.

Gary Slawther has acquired problem solving skills through periods of change where he has added value to the financing and financial risk management of businesses. At OCTAL, he has developed a robust treasury function and now occupies a strategic position to structure and source both debt and equity financing for this ambitious, high-growth business. Gary has developed an indepth knowledge of the commercial operations of the businesses to ensure that the risks and cash flows are understood and that the financing is appropriate; not least ensuring the adequacy of working capital and liquidity. There is also a requirement to blend that with the strategic direction of the business so that plans can be fulfilled. Gary's career has included financing of the supply chain, with the necessary understanding of the physical supply chain. This includes financing of raw materials, inventory, and receivables.

14

Leadership Is Leveraging the Full Output of Your People

John P. (Jack) Miles

Summary

Connecting performance with objectives through the use of metrics requires perfect alignment if it is to work across all functions. Sometimes, however, organizations don't fully leverage the talent and knowledge sitting within their own walls. Whether the need is improving finance's performance or better rotating talent within the organization, the answer is more communications, increased expectations, and circular accountability.

In this interview, Jack shares his consultative and collaborative model for how he would go about exploring and developing the finance function based on a deep cross-functional understanding. He approaches linking the finance function with the customer facing units of the business from a background in procurement and general leadership.

Interview with John P. (Jack) Miles conducted June 30, 2016

There has to be a particularly tight connection between procurement and finance for a whole host of reasons, not the least of which is how 'savings' is defined and what the organization finds to be an acceptable benchmark for the metric.

There are a few things that I would start with when detailing a plan for improving how finance works. Firstly, I'd understand what their key operating measures and their performance metrics are and how they report them. Most importantly, frankly, is how they count them, because it's great to have measures,

J.P. (Jack) Miles
MainSpring Advisors, Winter Park, FL, USA

© The Author(s) 2018
M. Lind, K. Barner, *Finance Unleashed*, DOI 10.1007/978-3-319-66370-8_14

Setting the foundation to understand
how to link the finance functions

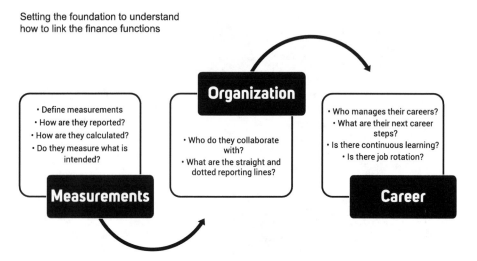

Fig. 14.1 Understanding how the finance function works as a foundation to break down silos and re-focus. Connect measurements with the organization and each individual career

yet it's interesting when you start to dive into exactly how we calculate those measures. Sometimes, the formula or the manner in which we measure them doesn't really provide the outcomes that you might expect to receive.

Secondly, I would study the collaboration and interaction with various parts of the organization. If it's a shared services type of function, how do the finance people within those departments or divisions report up the chain? Are they direct reports to the business heads or is it a dotted line approach?

Thirdly, the most important, who manages the finance person's career? Is he or she in a business group, a subsidiary, reporting up to the corporate financial organization? Personally, I could see that as a detriment because it negates the potential for that individual to be able to move into various places in the organization. From a collaborative relationship or a career growth standpoint, they could find themselves at a dead end in that company unless they actively pursue something else. I believe it's really important to strike a balance between having people in roles where they understand what's going on, and also rotating them through different parts of the organization for them to get a broader career experience. When somebody's been in a position for two or three years, they've probably done all they're going to do. I would take a look at that holistically and then say, we'll try to understand how that finance organization is functioning within the overall organization.

Rotation is something that we discuss often, especially in finance. It is easy to get 'stuck' and become a finance expert. Who should be responsible for making this a practical reality?

I would look to the Human Resources (HR) organization to address this more than any other function – and they will have to make some changes if the rotation is designated as a priority. HR has historically had somewhat of a tendency to pigeonhole people based on their functional experience as opposed to their core competencies. I believe the core competencies and attributes of any particular role are usually more important to look at than the job title or the degree that somebody holds.

Consider organizations that actively and purposefully move people around. That mobility becomes part of how they operate and an expected part of each person's career path. It can be problematic if people are allowed to stagnate professionally. You will see the impact of that appear in individual and organizational performance scores. You can stagnate as an organization if you stop providing people with career opportunities. If the company is not working to advance their people, then it is not helping them grow and develop.

When you are running a finance organization, it is even more critical to resist the pull of stagnation because of the nature of the job. Leadership teams need to bring in new, fresh sets of eyes from time to time because once somebody is in a role for a period of time, they have a tendency to do things the way they've always been done. In fact, the longer someone is in a role, things have a way of coming full cycle and reaching the point where you would need them to change things they were responsible for establishing in the first place.

There are other steps you could take to improve the alignment between metrics and organizational effectiveness. I would take the key operating measures and go out and meet with the constituents and see how they are performing against those measures. After that, the next step is to have a conversation with the CEO and a couple of people from the board about their overall perception of finance. For instance, it is good to hear directly from them what they see as strengths or development opportunities and what challenges they see relative to the way the finance organization currently interacts with others. After that, it is probably necessary to take a deeper dive into your findings and confront key staff with them, even if this means having very open conversations, the results of which cannot be shared because you don't want to expose anyone. This is the only way to get a full and honest understanding of the finance organization and how it is performing.

How we most effectively measure finance's performance presents a challenge because it requires a level of subjectivity – even in the process of measurement. Certain things will be more important to some people than others, but I recommend starting each conversation about performance with a core set of the same questions. People can always expand and talk about other things, but there is a core group of topics that must be talked about with everyone.

How does finance feel about advancement opportunities? How do they feel about training and development? How do they feel about communications? These are critical questions to ask consistently of everyone involved.

The best way to have this kind of conversation, in my opinion, is to break it into two parts. Part one is a structured discussion resulting in data that you can correlate and turn into actionable information. Part two is about collecting the thoughts and general ideas that are on people's minds. What I've found when doing this in the past is that people usually have more in common than not. Once you have met with three or four people, you have a core group of things that you might not find on your list from part one of the conversation. Those things – which did not have their root in existing performance data – might be the things most likely to make people engage.

As an interviewer, your level of experience while conducting interviews affects what you learn. Interviewing requires a balance of art and science. You should avoid starting the process as though you already know it all. The more conversations you have, and the more similar the feedback is, the harder it is to play a little bit, not dumb exactly, but to ask questions and allow people to lead you through a unique conversation. There's typically much more that is the same in an organization than there are things that are different. That tendency usually makes itself obvious after a few conversations.

Most organizations I've had experience with are good at discovery and information gathering. They'll allow someone to go out and do that. The next part is turning that information into something actionable that they can take back to senior leadership. Most of the time there is a lot of head nodding that goes on at this point, because they all kind of agree to it. The third part, where we can put in multiple levers, is actually doing something about what we've learned. It's basically setting up an action plan to say, this is what we're seeing, this is what we're hearing, both of which are generally confirmed by the people in the organization. Assuming there are opportunities for improvement, we have to ask ourselves what we are going to do to bring about change and on what timeline?

The follow-up is often crucial here. We can come back to the old saying: *tell them what you're going to tell them – tell them – and then tell them what you told them.* It's going in and finding out what needs to be done and then articulating the vision. It's about having an action plan, and once the action plan is put in place, circling back and validating the progress that is being made or not being made and the perception or reality on the part of the people. To me this is where a lot of us have the opportunity to improve because people will want to do something, but they don't necessarily do it. For instance: reporting back to the troops around what's been said and the feedback that we've gotten from all of them.

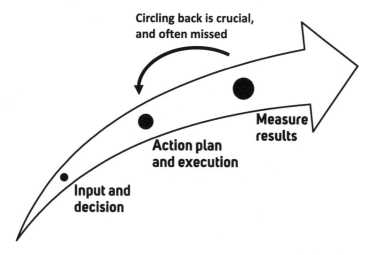

Fig. 14.2 The three steps to measure results. Continuous circling back to revise in an interactive way is sometimes rare, yet crucial, to get the change you aspire

Here's the reaction of the management, of the leadership team, and here is what they're going to commit to doing to make some of the changes and start to pivot the organization in a different direction. Then you ask people if the changes are really being made and continue to circle back and tell them what you're going to do. This is probably the most important success factor.

Consider when companies do periodic employee surveys. Many times, if you look in the rear-view mirror at several of them, you find that employees are saying the same thing over and over again despite the fact that nothing changes. Successful companies go out and get that survey information and they communicate what the results are. The leadership team commits to making changes and then circles back to the employees on some of the changes they've made and asks them to validate whether, in fact, it made a difference.

How we will succeed to make a functional organization, like finance, agree to work more cross-functionally has to do with the principles the organization is based on. I've found that those mandates typically come from the CFO and are affected by each person's management flexibility.

I worked in an organization where a new CFO came on board and was totally driven by days payable outstanding, or DPO. We had terms and conditions in there for our suppliers and we pretty much paid within the terms and conditions. The CFO wanted to see a DPO that was probably 90–100 days. Well, clearly, it created a conflict, because if we have terms and conditions with our suppliers, we've got to operate that way. There are other ways to set it up where you can have variability around payment terms with some of the suppliers, and you also have to take a look at what's being purchased and what's being procured. If you're talking about labor; people aren't going to wait 90–100 days to get paid. I mean, this is direct evidence of the organizational philosophy.

You also could factor in what kind of business you're in by how you can promote cross-functional cooperation. For instance, I think there are big differences between manufacturing and services environments. In manufacturing, there are typically pretty good specifications defining what is required. They've gone into it with a level of detail. Many times, the one thing that's a variable is the amount of collaboration that takes place between the suppliers and the manufacturer or the assembler.

In a services environment, you don't have the same level of precision in the specifications. That is one of the reasons, frankly, that supply chain and procurement people that have worked within a manufacturing environment sometimes have a challenging time migrating to a services environment. They're used to very specific and detailed information on exactly what they want to do and having a good set of requirements. On the services side, you typically don't have that and in the long term you may wind up paying more for a product because suppliers have to build in contingencies for things that they were not aware of.

Another important fact is knowing how to hire someone, which actually isn't really complicated. What it goes back to is what we talked about before related to people rotating in jobs. Ask yourself: "What are their skills? What are their competencies? What are the attributes that are needed for the job? What's the match-up? Where are the shortages? Where are the deficiencies? Where are some of the things that they have to work on?" When you sit down and work on it that way, your focus will be on their skills, competencies, and attributes rather than someone that you think has done the job (or one similar to it) before.

Good leaders and good managers can do that. You know where people have their strengths. You know what they do well. You know how they react. You know how they don't react and when they step up. Those are the things that leadership should focus on as they have performance conversations with folks. You tell them what they need to work on, where they need to grow, and how they should be thinking about becoming well rounded enough for their next job rotation or their next position. Leadership requires a lot of mentorship and that can give good returns if done well and consistently. Leadership is about leveraging the output of your people.

There are a few companies out there that do this exceptionally well. I worked with a company that had a lot of government contracts which required us to work with minority suppliers. We had to report to the government every quarter on our use of minority suppliers and we had a handful of things that we could easily get and we worked through some intermediaries sometimes to be able to get it. I remember having a conversation with the CFO about having to pay the minority suppliers a little more. These are hard things to deal with and a finance organization has to be extremely careful about what they do, and – more importantly – how they do it, understanding the impact and ramifications of the policies they put in place. If you're dealing with a product that's very price sensitive, where every couple of pennies counts, and you're going to push a DPO plan out to 90 or 100 days from 30 days, you need to accept that your price points are going to change.

To ensure the finance department uses optimal measures, you need to open up the picture to the entire organization and all the other value propositions. That means finance people should be good at collaborating and interacting and working together with the businesses to create those measures. You have to clearly define what problems you want to solve. Is it a cash flow problem? An issue of costs or volumes? Or do we need to decrease working capital? There's a really interesting dynamic when collaboration works, and it clearly takes a bunch of people working together as well as the voice of reason.

The finance organization can come closer to understanding the customer by 'healing' themselves. There are many finance organizations that interact and collaborate very well with the rest of the business. But there are also some that don't. This often comes down to basic management principles. How do you get the right skills, competencies, structural organizational set-up, and attributes in an organization to accomplish the overall business objectives? Some of that sends a message to the organization, and some of it becomes a command and control thing. I've always believed in a strategy where the finance people in an organization have a primary reporting line into the CEO and a secondary reporting relationship to the line of business. That way you wind up with better controls as finance strives to serve two masters, mirroring the complexity of the finance organization itself.

Conclusion

Companies talk about breaking down silos and enabling cross-functional alignment, yet what they often do in the normal course of operations actually reinforces segmentation. Initiatives such as shared metrics, organizational rotation, and deliberate career management can improve output as well as the level of innovation the organization is capable of. Finance is at particularly high risk of stagnation due to the structured nature of the job.

Finance becomes better aligned with customer value when open discussions (or internal interviews) take place, leading to the development of formal action plans, and resulting in regular follow up. For this reason, it is important for the CFO to have a primary reporting line into the CEO and a secondary reporting relationship to the line of business.

Key Take-Aways

- In order for metrics to result in the performance they were established to deliver, it is important for leaders to scrutinize how they are calculated and what activities they drive.
- The key to ensuring people create tangible value is focusing on their skills and talent rather than their past job titles.
- HR has an important role to play. Besides placing individuals in open positions, HR must also prepare them for their next roles as their current positions transform or expire. Employees, managers, and leadership share the responsibility to make this happen.
- Good leaders and managers are able to see beyond job titles to relevant skills, competencies and attributes. Helping people apply their talent in alternative roles can be more fulfilling and bring much needed objectivity and results.
- Measuring what you want to improve is a given. Circling back feedback containing actions from results and new expectations is equally important. It is critical to communicate and then inspect what you expect!

Jack Miles is Former Chief Procurement Officer for top organizations in Canada and the United States, including Canadian Imperial Bank of Commerce (CIBC), American International Group (AIG), Cigna, Computer Associates, Ames Department Stores, and Prentice Hall. Jack was also appointed Secretary of The Florida Department of Management Services by Governor Scott and served in that role until 2012. Jack is a sought-after advisor and leader, known for his experience and reputation for developing and successfully executing business strategies and his ability to deliver operational excellence and benchmark performance in functions which typically underperform in most companies. He is an entrepreneurial executive adept at turn-around situations and building businesses, both international and domestic. His key attributes include creative strategic thinking, and his demonstrated operational capabilities in the development of organizations.

15

Financial and Operational Measurements

Luis Manuel Hernandez

Summary

We reached out to Luis Manuel Hernandez, PhD, to learn how he uses supply chain methodologies such as Lean Manufacturing and Six Sigma to improve the finance function. His Lean Six Sigma approach is critical to our thesis since it focuses the entire organization on the value they create for end-customers and it also leads to clear and decisive priorities. All of the actions we take that are benefiting our customers are value-added. In this case, and as measured through quality standards, Lean and Six Sigma help us stay on course and avoid getting distracted by company politics or bureaucracy, neither of which have direct value to customers. Here Luis explains his Lean Six Sigma model for finance.

Interview with Luis Manuel Hernandez conducted June 30, 2016

I have studied accounting and manufacturing and have worked to connect our understanding of what is happening on the shop floor and linking that to company financials. There are usually some gaps in those links in the reporting. This affects the accuracy of the picture that financial data paints to management and how they use it for the decisions they make from it.

For a number of years, there has been a drive to make the finance function as a whole – and the CFO in particular – improve their business acumen beyond the areas of reporting and regulatory skills. Their expanded capabilities have largely been driven by the inclusion of two new techniques. The first one

L.M. Hernandez, Ph.D.
Mexico's National Manufacturing Industry Council,
Tijuana, Mexico

is Six Sigma, which is a disciplined, data-driven methodology for eliminating defects in any process, and the second one is Lean Manufacturing, which aims at the elimination of waste in every area of a process or a product. Both of these methodologies have been proven to be very good tools for improving the connection between the finance function and the actual performance of the company in terms of the total value created for customers.

The starting point is the fact that a commercial business is the sum of the interactions between customers, suppliers, and competitors. Their interactions are constantly evolving and are typically measured using indicators that don't always translate well into traditional finance metrics. The reason for this disconnect is that finance professionals are usually working at a distance – either geographically or organizationally – from where things are happening (aka *Gemba*, which is Japanese for 'the real place', or where the value is created).

One metric we can use to connect finance with "the real place" is On Time Delivery (OTD), which measures what percentage of the goods ordered by each customer are actually provided. At an OTD of 100 percent, we ensure that all of our customer's needs are met. This metric is effective because it is simple and translates easily into parallel financial metrics: sales appear in the income statement, accounts receivable are increased, and there are traceable inflows and outflows of cash. When OTD is not fulfilled (meaning any sustained percentage of less than 100 percent), it will, over time, be possible to see a deterioration of sales and how the collections decrease, resulting in lower cash flows – which sooner or later affect both purchasing and profitability. This predictive element of OTD therefore simultaneously connects the finances of the business with their operational performance and provides an early indicator that decisions makers can respond to.

The other metric that we have introduced in the context of Lean and Six Sigma is quality as a key figure for measuring the effectiveness of a given process as a percentage against a pre-established target. When quality is below 100 percent, we can expect that sales, costs, receivables, inventory, cash outflow, and non-cash items will deteriorate as well. We use Yield as the quality measure that compares the ratio of inputs to outputs and correlates to the income statement, balance sheet, and cash flows of the company. In the example below we relate a hypothetical company's quality performance to financial terms. The Yield compares the input of 400 units to the output of 375 (93.75 percent), which financially translates to that we planned to earn $1,200 and realized $1,125 instead. The cost of poor quality to the company was therefore $75, appearing on the income statement as lower sales, unaffected costs, and a deteriorating cash flow.

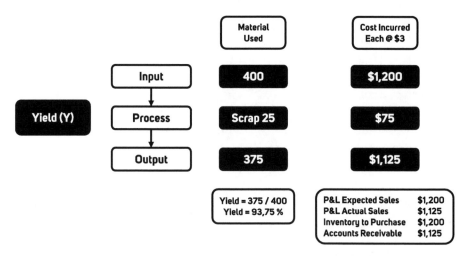

Fig. 15.1 An example of how using On Time Delivery (OTD) can measure yield as a prediction of how the financial results will develop

Conclusion

Luis Manuel Hernandez clearly presents how accounting and finance are not producing optimal value if they cannot translate into customer value.

One of the strengths of Luis' formula is that it is based on a notion of how much is sold v. delivered on-time: a customer-centric metric. Although we may talk about finance needing to take a more customer-centric view, we really need customer value to be placed at the center of the organization and for all functions to align around it. We should allow small tolerance for discrepancies between reported and actual results.

A commercial business is the sum of the interactions between customers, suppliers, and competitors. Their interactions are evolving constantly and are typically measured using indicators that don't always translate well into traditional finance metrics.

Key Take-Aways

- Financial accounting was not developed with the customer in mind, and accounting principles have pushed it even further away from the *Gemba* (Japanese for the real place, or where the value is created).
- Measuring On Time Delivery (OTD) is a method that improves the connection between finance and *Gemba* while providing good indicators of quality and customer value creation.

- Quality is measured as Yield, comparing input versus output and ultimately translates into the income statement and cash flow.
- When management is based on reports that are created away from operations, organizations are at risk of making decisions based on incomplete or non-representative data.
- By implementing Lean and Six Sigma in accounting, companies can bring their operation into alignment with finance by prioritizing the elimination of waste and defects.

Luis Manuel Hernandez, Ph.D. has developed Six Sigma financials and Lean Manufacturing financials at Tecnologico Monterrey, the largest technical university in Mexico. Luis has taught MBA students throughout Mexico as well as in California and Arizona.

Part III

Implications

"There is only one boss. The customer. And he can fire everybody in the company from the chairman on down, simply by spending his money somewhere else."
– Sam Walton

Introduction

Finance is a corporate function with a strategic future extending far beyond their tactical, operational roots. That said, finance leaders are in a position to make meaningful changes today with the ideas and inspiration to go from here to there, making finance a factor driving competitiveness and customer engagement and therefore relevant to the CEO and the board.

Transformational CFOs are attuned to 'the bigger picture' of enterprise objectives and can analyze how trends, including the rise of customer-centricity, are likely to affect their role and priorities. There are many positive implications of viewing the financial supply chain in parallel to the physical chain, and when the entire C-suite (with the CFO in a leading position) shares a customer-centric focus, they can continue to build on the advantages of the 'ecosystem play'.

In the third section of this book, we pull together the central concepts from Part I and the key take-aways from our influencer interviews in Part II. We start by painting a big picture and putting financial supply chain transformation into a larger context. We will identify mega-trends, present suggestions for how the CFO can implement customer-centricity, and optimize the financial supply chain, all so finance can initiate innovation and foster the 'ecosystem play'.

16

The Context

Magnus Lind and Kelly Barner

The Big Picture

Darwin taught us that the key to survival is adaptability to change. Does this mean that the banks will die out like the dinosaurs, modern behemoths unfit for new times? Will they be unbundled and killed off by fintech start-ups? Given how established they are, perhaps we should stop considering whether banks are good for the financial ecosystem (or not) and instead study how they fit into the financial supply chain.

The primary purpose of the banks is to fund the government directly as well as indirectly via real estate and private households. This has been an underlying theme in all financial regulations (especially by current regulatory regimes) passed since the 1980's.[1] The intent of these regulations is not to decrease the level of debt in the economy or to fund the corporate sector, but to ensure that the government always has access to the cheapest cash, either because the banks (including the central banks) buy their bonds and debt papers or through financing households so they can continue to consume and pay taxes. This is also why real estate has always been favored by financial regulation; it funnels taxes to the government when the private sector borrows to build. There is nothing like a real estate bubble to improve the government's financial standing, until the bubble bursts of course. Then the bankers are to blame – or so we are told.

M. Lind
Skanor Group Ltd, London, UK

K. Barner
Buyers Meeting Point, Shrewsbury, MA, USA

© The Author(s) 2018
M. Lind, K. Barner, *Finance Unleashed*, DOI 10.1007/978-3-319-66370-8_16

As a result of all this, the banks cannot be made to disappear; they are integral to the financial system as a whole. Meanwhile, fintech companies are 'only' considered to be a technical layer because they do not provide foundational funding. Many times they operate on top of bank or credit card company infrastructures, like PayPal.[2] It would be farfetched to expect banks to be replaced by a fragmented plethora of fintech companies that supplement rather than supersede the bank's primary function.

The corporate sector is not prioritized in financial regulations. It has always been regarded as high risk, and therefore something for banks to more or less avoid. This is why access to corporate loans fluctuates so much with the economic cycle.

Small and medium-sized businesses have already experienced dis-intermediation from the banking system because of the harsh policies and regulations implemented since 2008. This is in line with long-term regulatory strategies; it has forced corporates to adjust their business models so they rely on sources of financing other than the banks. This primarily affects the small companies in each supply chain, the ones that often are business-critical and that participate in the process of innovation, helping larger enterprises protect against the risk of being disrupted by current and new competitors.

This dis-intermediation will likely be continued in the next crisis, which, judging from current debt levels, becomes more probable every day.[3] From 2008 to 2016, the central banks used most of the available options to stimulate the economy. If a new crisis happens too soon, there are few additional measures left for them to employ in response. They have already established zero percent interest rates, printed loads of money, initiated massive bond-buying schemes (quantitative easing), and allowed governments to operate with record deficits (in the USA at least) in an effort to stimulate recovery.

Another big picture trend is the de-globalization (or regionalization) of the banks. Charlie Bean presents the logic behind this trend in Chapter 12, "However we should expect many banks retreating to their domestic markets would be one of the consequences of the financial crisis. It's effectively a de-globalization of finance that partly reflects the fact that banks typically know more about their domestic markets than they do know about foreign markets. Often where banks end up coming unstuck is by engaging in foreign ventures that they don't properly understand."

This unintentional regionalization means that global corporations need to enter into an abundance of bank relationships, the minority of which will be core institutions that provide financing, back-up credit facilities, and cash management services. Most of the banking relationships are non-core, only providing localized services like payroll and tax payments. Forming and maintaining so many separate banking relationships leads to extra costs with little added benefit beyond being able to operate in a specific region. In addition, local adjustments to payment and collection processes increase the risk of payment and ecommerce fraud.[4] The regionalization of the banks ultimately leads to suboptimal use of cash and makes it more expensive to concentrate available cash for optimal use by the business.

Banking fragmentation has already created demand for international financial services that are layered on top of the banks. Although these layered solutions are more cohesive offerings, they still add extra costs. Customers that want to make international purchases seem prepared to let merchants pay extra for services like payments and funding if they can work with a one-stop-shop supplier. PayPal is a good example of a provider who can accept and send payments nearly anywhere, and, as a result, PayPal is able to charge massive fees for this service.[5] Since banks are effectively prohibited from providing 'global' services that 'global' customers require, CFOs are presented with an opportunity to offer this to their corporate customers, exactly as UPS and DHL have done and as we describe in Chapter 11.

Another consequence of bank regionalization is that it inhibits their ability to deliver anything but intermittent trade finance solutions on a global basis. This likely means that when we transition from regarding the financial supply chain as a series of independent links to seeing it as interdependent links that form one chain, the banks will no longer be able to take the same leading role. The banks will continue to be important, but secondary, and they will be restricted to providing financing, investment services, and financial infrastructure. We would require solutions able to coordinate several banks to provide a full chain solution. Historically, the banks have met this demand by developing a network of 'correspondent' banks to provide services outside their jurisdiction. The future of the correspondent banking system remains unknown. If that system could be made more seamless and efficient it would be able to compete with third-party overlay solutions that connect multiple regional banks and provide a single-point-of-contact.

When the banks prioritize the health of the public sector over private sector growth, corporate leadership teams should look to their own abilities to fund and manage financial risk in the supply chain. Given that this may be a new realization for many companies, they must ask the following question: How can my company build up the financial supply chain and optimize capital allocation instead of relying upon the banking system to do it for us? Or, putting it another way, is it time to merge my physical supply chain with my financial supply chain?

The fact that banks are likely to survive financial sector disruption doesn't necessarily mean that there won't be any changes in the way they operate. When we reach the point where banks and fintech companies are operating side by side, there is likely to be some cross-pollination, providing an opportunity for business savvy CFOs.

The Role of the Central Banks Became Central

When the international financial crisis, triggered by the collapse of the investment bank Lehman Brothers, hit with full force in September of 2008, a long period of global bank expansion came to an end. Relationships between corporations and banks came under strain, in some cases leading to the end of decades-old relationships. The great liquidity squeeze that followed the crisis in 2008 and continued well into 2010–2011, taught the corporate sector a lesson: do not rely on too few funding sources: diversify. Ensure that you have sufficient cash on hand at all times, deleveraging if necessary.

The financial crisis created a new role for the central banks, a central economic policy role in fact. Since the economic problem was exacerbated by high indebtedness and low liquidity, no one other than the central banks could fix the problem. Their extraordinary response activities (printing money, providing low interest rates, buying bonds, etc.) positioned them as leaders in fixing the economy. This was a new situation for the central bank governors.

At the end of September 2008 (two weeks after the Lehman Brothers debacle), a roundtable of treasurers turned into a therapy session where person after person shared his or her depressing story. They could not access their money from money market funds. One company was in the process of bridge financing a US$500 million acquisition (which they considered minor) and had only managed to gather US$1 million (!) from a large American household bank. Not even the banks could find funding. The whole situation was surreal and it didn't get better in the first half of 2009. The central banks and other policy makers were unprepared, as they had not developed a toolbox for this type of situation. On the other hand, some central banks were quick to grasp the situation. The Bank of England, for instance, started to offer different kinds of direct lending to corporates having substantial operations in the UK in 2009. It became an important lifeline for many.[6,7]

At the beginning of the crisis, most central banks and policy makers were unaware of what was really happening in the corporate sector. At the time, the central banks were much more bank-centric than they are today. You could almost say monetary policies were rolled out through the banks, who were expected to translate them to the real economy without the central bank intervening. The central banks only interacted with other banks; this was their modus operandi, one that had worked well for decades. The financial crisis changed this model. All central banks now have regular meetings with corporate leaders so they can follow developments in the private sector more closely and better understand how policies unravel in the real economy. This has led to policy makers making decisions with improved understanding and perspective than in the past. The central bank governors have come out of their ivory towers.

A recent (albeit underdiscussed) milestone in corporate understanding of the financial supply chain was a speech given by Mario Draghi, president of the European Central Bank (ECB), in March of 2017[8] at a joint conference with the US-based MIT Lab for Innovation Science and Policy.[9] The conference was called "Fostering Innovation and Entrepreneurship in the Euro area" and was held in Frankfurt, Germany. In his speech, Draghi addressed innovation, adoption of innovation, and productivity.

In his opening address, Mario said:

> [Innovation] might at first glance seem an unusual topic for a central bank conference, since monetary policy principally operates through the demand side of the economy. But the long-term supply picture evidently also affects our ability to deliver on our mandate... aggregate productivity growth is more than just the development and application of innovation and new technologies which enhance or even revolutionize production processes. New technologies invented elsewhere need to be adapted by firms into their own production processes to make them more efficient. In short, productivity growth depends not only on the creation of new ideas, but also on their diffusion. To raise productivity growth, which has slowed in the euro area and in many other economies in recent years, we need to focus on both areas.[10]

Customer-Centric Financial Regulation

Disruption in the form of technology and new financial regulations is carving out a different role for the banks that effectively restricts their direct support of the real economy. Meanwhile, there are several good initiatives from governments pushing for faster innovation in finance.

The Federal Reserve is spearheading the 'Faster Payments Task Force' which aims to achieve real-time domestic payments in the USA.[11] In the European Union (EU), the first 'Payment Service Directive' (PSD), which aims to boost innovations in the payment area, was adopted in 2007. The most notable result has been the 'Single Euro Payments Area' (SEPA) allowing for close to real-time payments of euros within the EU, including even the EU countries that retained their national currencies, such as Sweden and Denmark. The SEPA has effectively eliminated 'cross-border' euro payments within and between EU member states since all payments in euros within the EU are now treated as domestic payments.

In 2018, the next version of the PSD (PSD2) is rolled out in the EU. It forces banks and so-called Payment Service Providers (e.g., Ayden, Klarna, and PayPal) to give access to their customers' accounts to allow transactions ordered at the customer's request. The security requirements will be rigorous. The advantages of PSD2 are significant as it allows the implementation of layers of payment solutions that are bank agnostic, providing CFOs with improved efficiencies, oversight and payment statistics, and security, and creates more opportunities to innovate.[12]

"Stop Pushing Payment Terms, Pay Promptly!" Demands the Government

Initiatives to curb the practice of pushing payment terms are being implemented in more and more countries to ensure that large companies do not misuse their dominant position relative to smaller suppliers. Governments (and central banks) have realized that the largest source of new job creation is small and medium-sized businesses (SMBs). SMBs frequently complain of late payments and claim that a shortage of cash stifles their ability to grow. There are several initiatives effectively attacking the 'working capital dogma' in the sense of pushing 'Days Payable Outstanding' (DPO). Many of these well-meaning initiatives are voluntary rather than being put into law, allowing the corporate sector to self-regulate.

In the USA, President Obama introduced the 'SupplierPay' pledge in 2014.[13] The Netherlands has Betaalme.nu (English: 'Paymenow')[14] a not-for-profit initiative that aims to ease SMB supplier access to reasonably-priced liquidity. Betaalme.nu is supported and subsidized by the Dutch Ministry for Economic Affairs. The UK has initiated the 'Prompt Payment Code' which has participating companies agree to: (1) pay suppliers on time; (2) give clear guidance to suppliers (including procedures for complaints and disputes, and prompt advice of late payments and the reasons); and (3) encourage good practice (which means that the suppliers shall encourage the code in their own supply chains).[15]

These initiatives provide direction to finance executives working to take a supply chain view and foster cooperation and financial innovation in the eco-system. Add the banks' dis-intermediation to the corporate sector with their abundance of cash and credit, and you may find gaps in the offerings where you can innovate to remain competitive. This disruption is happening in the remit of the CFO and the CEO and provides them with the opportunity to develop new customer value propositions.

Big Picture Conclusions for CFOs

- The global debt situation is not favorable, drawing many warnings from the IMF and others on the combination of increased indebtedness and low productivity growth. CFOs, CEOs, and boards should consider engaging in scenario and mitigation planning for another liquidity crisis and its possible effects on the supply chain.
- Financing the corporate sector is a residual rather than a fundamental role of the financial system. Instead, the financial system exists to fund governments, real estate, and households, which is the reason bank lending to corporates fluctuates so much.
- Banking will remain regionalized, meaning that funding a global financial supply chain will require overlays and multi-institutional coordination. This presents CFOs with the opportunity to provide financial support to their customers in a seamless, borderless fashion.
- During the financial crisis, the role of the central banks changed and they took the helm to turn the economy around with exceptional measures.
- Policy makers closely follow the rate of innovation and productivity which may cause them to pass new supportive policies. Implementing the innovation of other parties is a preferred approach to grow the economy and increase productivity.
- New financial regulations in the payments area allow greater innovation by providing overlay solutions. This will also create an incentive for banks to provide instant payments, even across borders.
- Pushing payment terms onto suppliers will draw more scrutiny than in the past. Governments have realized that the potential for job growth lies with small and medium-sized businesses and that prompt payment is a good and necessary solution for increasing employment.

The Drill and the Kill, or the 'Ecosystem Fight'

The legacy practice of pushing capital and capital costs up and down the chain has led to finance spending considerable time and resources 'window dressing' the balance sheet while risking the increase of actual capital costs and the amount of capital tied up in other parts of the chain. This can negatively affect the customer experience and lead to higher costs that diminish competitiveness.

This 'drill', as we call it, may lead your company into the 'kill' where the supply chain is starved for free cash, unable to innovate sufficiently, and forced to fight for survival month after month with razor-thin margins, low availability of cash, and a high cost of capital. Eventually, a suboptimal financial supply chain may lead to it being disrupted by newcomers that take advantage of the precarious situation the short-term winners have created.

In the short to medium term, suboptimal capital allocation in the financial supply chain may be successful, at least for the companies that employ it on purpose. In fact, those who manage to push working capital up and down the supply chain often perform best in profit and share price. Their CEOs and CFOs are celebrated and very well remunerated since the share value increases and the company can pay more dividends. The working capital dogma seems to be effective in the medium term and supports a focus aligned with the current perspective of most corporate managers and investors. But how resilient does it make a company (and the ecosystem as a whole) to external disruption over time?

The negative effects of pushing working capital up and down the supply chain emerge over the long term, since it assumes a fairly static market focused on incremental product improvements and gradual increases in market penetration. In other words, it assumes a 'business as usual' environment. A focus on working capital reduction does not take the impact of disruptive innovation into consideration, regardless of the source. An overly fundamentalist approach to hitting working capital targets can be detrimental in the face of a constantly increasing risk of disruption.

A typical example of this would be a company that built its success out of one or more disruptive innovations and gained enormous growth and success. During the period when the company addressed new types of customer demand, it drove the market, created new products, built a large customer base, and managed to increase margins, eventually amassing huge piles of cash. This places them in a market leading position – a pleasant spot to be in and naturally important to protect once achieved – even when the rate of new product launches, profit generation, and cash flow declines. The company institutes professional management of the incremental improvements when its successful products and disruptive innovation stalls. Often, when a company reaches this position, it is forced to start defending its place in the ecosystem. It even risks becoming complacent and taking on a sense of entitlement.

The company may introduce bureaucracy and rules to protect itself, resisting disruptive innovation and even becoming a 'Big Fat Cat': slow in mind, body, and reflexes. Even a hungry baby tiger could eat it alive. The average lifespan of an S&P Index company has decreased from more than 60 years at the end of the 1950s to less than 20 years today.[16],[17] This is a clear warning against allowing short-term financial targets to rule a company's long-term strategy and vision. It also spotlights the necessity for finance and the board to

Decay of Working Capital Dogma

The KPI

$$\frac{EBITDA}{Working\ Capital}$$

The DRILL
1. CFO pushes CPO on DPO
2. CPO pushes supply chain
3. Suppliers suffer
4. Increased risks
5. Reduced innovation
6. Treasurer doesn't know where to invest the cash

The KILL
1. Generating lion share of cash and profits in the demand and supply chain
2. Complacency and sense of entitlement
3. "Big Fat Cat Syndrome"
4. Introducing conserving bureaucracy
5. Resistance to disruptive innovation and disturbing the (comfortable) status quo

Fig. 16.1 The Drill and the Kill caused by narrow-minded working capital targets. Unfortunately, in the short term pushing working capital usually produces winners, while opening the ecosystem to disruption in the long term

set metrics and targets that correspond to a much more strategic understanding than singular balance sheet capital targets.

By highlighting the need for finance with an end-customer focus, the company will understand how their metrics and finance processes affect competitiveness and their ability to service their current and future customer base. It will also withdraw from the silo mentality found in many Big Fat Cats.

The working capital target gives rise to 'the drill' (Fig. 16.1). The board forces the CFO to expand the Days Payables Outstanding (DPO) metric by pushing supplier payments out – often in a brutal and heavy-handed way. Regardless of whether the company receives a supplier's goods and services on day D, the supplier shall get paid in D+30, +60, +90, +120 days or even later. Supply Chain Finance (SCF) was developed to address the risk of suppliers defaulting from a liquidity squeeze by allowing large buying companies to offer contacts with banks or finance providers to discount the supplier's invoice based on the credit rating of the buyer. SCF does solve an important consequence of the working capital dogma, but it is the dogma that is the problem. SCF solves a symptom rather than addressing the root cause.

There are reasons other than working capital targets that the lifespan of S&P Index companies has decreased. However, we address the working capital targets repeatedly since they are so ingrained and introduce an attitude that is not customer-centric. Companies could be exposing themselves to disruptive innovation by building up rigid structures. If nothing else, this is definitely more of a destructive 'ecosystem fight' than a productive 'ecosystem play'. Innosight,[18] the company behind Fig. 16.2, refers to Richard Foster and Sarah Kaplan in their book *Creative Destruction*.[19] According to Foster and Kaplan, the lifespan of a corporation is determined "…by balancing three management imperatives:

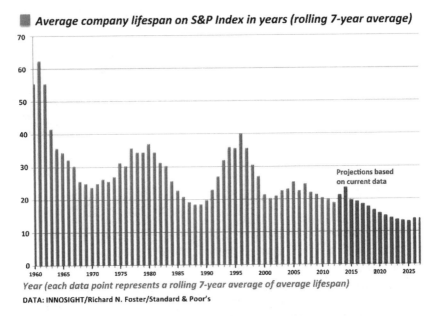

■ *Average company lifespan on S&P Index in years (rolling 7-year average)*

Year (each data point represents a rolling 7-year average of average lifespan)

DATA: INNOSIGHT/Richard N. Foster/Standard & Poor's

Fig. 16.2 This graph (and its predecessors) is famous in its own right, in part because its predictions have been so accurate. The lifespan of an average company on the S&P index has fallen by two-thirds since 1960, from almost 60 years to less than 20 in the second decade of this millennium. Data Innosight analysis based on public S&P 500 data sources

1) Running operations effectively,
2) Creating new businesses, which meet customer needs, and
3) Shedding business that once might have been core but now no longer meet company standards for growth and return."[20]

These management imperatives explain how CFOs can improve strategically together with the CEO by setting the right metrics and operating smoothly with a customer-centric supply chain view, supporting successful innovation and intelligently managing failed attempts at innovation.

The Physical Chain Transformation, or Industry 4.0

Many finance executives are already embracing the change stemming from developments in manufacturing and the physical supply chain. In our contacts with CFOs from multinational companies, we are told about many efforts that are made to modernize financing and align it with the new cyber-connected manufacturing Industry 4.0.

Industry	When	What
1.0	1790 →	Steam and water
2.0	1870 →	Assembly lines, electricity
3.0	1969 →	IT, automation
MIND THE GAP		
4.0	soon	IoT, cyber-connected supply chains

Fig. 16.3   The four industrial revolutions. Industry 1.0 was driven by advent of steam and water power at the turn of the eighteenth century. Industry 2.0 was built on division of labor, electricity, and the assembly lines at the turn of the twentieth century. Industry 3.0 used IT and robotics to automate manual processes, starting in the 1960s. The physical supply chain is currently taking the transformative step into Industry 4.0. The question is if the current financial supply chain supports or inhibits that transition. To all CFOs: Mind the Gap

Industry 4.0 was originated by the German government in 2011 and it is described as digitalized manufacturing and supply chain processes, connections of all 'things' (Internet of Things), and the use of sensors to steer and measure.[21] The core components of this movement include real-time monitoring and artificial intelligence where the production system automatically adjusts to disturbances and changes in demand.

Industry 4.0 requires substantial investments in software, hardware, and related services such as implementation, upgrades, support, and maintenance. These are types of investments that did not play a significant role in Industry versions 1–3 (Fig. 16.3 above) where the lion's share of production equipment took the form of manufacturing machines, factories, and resources for logistics. How will these new structural investments be financed and shared over the supply chain? Will investments override current corporate boundaries? How will cooperation over the supply chain be affected? Industry 4.0 includes 3-D printing with all its disruptive effects on capital and risk distribution among all the separate links in the supply chain.

Many CFOs are looking for ways to fund Industry 4.0 using asset finance, receivables, and supplier finance (for instance). Other opportunities lay in renting or leasing equipment or paying per produced unit. We believe the financial supply chain can take a quantum leap from today's opaque, batch-driven financial systems, mimicking and connecting to new manufacturing and supply chain solutions. The system's performance gaps from the current financial supply chain to Industry 4.0 may otherwise be too wide and might even hinder progress in the physical supply chain.

Replicating an Industry 4.0 mindset in the financial supply chain will bridge internal silos and even cross-company borders. Connecting finance targets and processes to the new, cyber-connected physical future is a task for business savvy CFOs, treasurers, and other finance executives.

Elementum[22] is an example of a physical supply chain platform that focuses on the output rather than the process. They accomplish this by providing real-time monitoring and suggested solutions to mitigate disruptions in real time. For instance, if ships are unable to enter a port because of a blockage of some kind, the system automatically finds an alternative and redirects the shipment. In doing so, the platform replaces a 'firefighting' management approach with a focus on progress: detecting trends, identifying improvements, and furthering the understanding of how to improve competitiveness.

The whole chain is monitored in real-time on large screens in a command center that is reminiscent of what you might see in a science fiction setting. This is the near future of managing the physical chain but still the long-term future for managing the financial chain. When considering the complexity of the physical (goods & services) versus the financial (data) chains, we realize that this situation is a paradox. How does a finance executive use this opportunity to their advantage? How well is your financial supply chain adjusted for Elementum-style models and visions? Can your financial supply chain even support Industry 4.0, or does it, in the worst case scenario, inhibit it?

In Industry 4.0, the supply chain automatically adapts to disturbances. Let's assume there is a ship on its way to a big assembly plant in Gothenburg, Sweden to offload components that will be put into products. The supply chain is managed just-in-time with no excess inventory. Now let's suppose there is a strike at the port of Gothenburg.[23] Under Industry 4.0, the ship will automatically be re-routed to another port and trucks will be scheduled to take the components from the new port directly to the assembly plant. This all happens without any human interaction and supply chain managers are able to follow the outcome on screens and through real-time reporting. The physical chain is delayed, yet it works seamlessly. The adjustments are made with navigator-like logic, responding without hesitation when a route is changed or the driver misses an exit: the system just recalculates.

How will the financial chain handle this altered routing? New invoices have to be issued, vendor data must be updated and verified, payment information needs to be updated and verified, etc., and much of this has to be done manually. The financial chain is hardly a seamless flow; it has a very low level of automation in comparison to current reality of the physical chain. The trucks from the new port have to be paid as one-off transactions and the trucks waiting at the port of Gothenburg have to be compensated with a different fee since they did not transport anything. The finance department gets busy firefighting and solves this through email, telephone, and maybe even telefax.

As illustrated in this example, the CFO does not lack opportunities to improve the financial supply chain, especially if the target is to migrate to Industry 4.0.

Notes

1. Treasury Peer, "Basel III for Dummies – How and Why it Hurts Corporates," YouTube Video, 8:09, Posted June 3, 2012, https://www.youtube.com/watch?v=_G6fprBPhss.
2. Ed Grabianowski and Stephanie Crawford, "How PayPal Works," *How Stuff Works*, December 13, 2005, http://money.howstuffworks.com/paypal2.htm.
3. Larry Elliott, "IMF Urges Governments to Tackle Record Global Debt of $152tn," *The Guardian*, October 5, 2016, https://www.theguardian.com/business/2016/oct/05/world-debt-has-hit-record-high-of-152tn-says-imf.
4. "Payment Fraud: What is it and How it Can Be Avoided?," *Big Commerce*, Accessed June 29, 2017, https://www.bigcommerce.com/ecommerce-answers/payment-fraud-what-it-and-how-it-can-be-avoided/.
5. J.P. Buntinx, "Using PayPal Becomes Far More Expensive Than Before Come March 29," *NewsBTC*, February 12, 2017, http://www.newsbtc.com/2017/02/12/using-paypal-becomes-far-expensive-come-march-29/.
6. Bank of England Asset Purchase Facility Fund Limited, "Annual Report 2009/10," *Bank of England*, Accessed June 29, 2017, http://www.bankofengland.co.uk/publications/Documents/other/markets/apf/boeapfannualreport1007.pdf.
7. Asset Purchase Facility, "Corporate Bond Secondary Market Scheme (2009–2016)," *Bank of England*, Accessed June 29, 2017, http://www.bankofengland.co.uk/markets/Pages/apf/corporatebond/default.aspx.
8. Mario Draghi, "Moving to the Frontier: Promoting the Diffusion of Innovation," *European Central Bank*, March 13, 2017, https://www.ecb.europa.eu/press/key/date/2017/html/sp170313_1.en.html.
9. "MIT Innovation Initiative," Accessed June 29, 2017, https://innovation.mit.edu.
10. Draghi, "Moving to the Frontier," *European Central Bank*.

11. "Federal Reserve System Appoints Faster Payments Strategy Leader," *The Federal Reserve*, July 30, 2015, https://www.federalreserve.gov/newsevents/pressreleases/other20150730a.htm.

12. "Payment Services Directive: Frequently Asked Questions," *European Commission*, October 8, 2015, http://europa.eu/rapid/press-release_MEMO-15-5793_en.htm?locale=en.

13. Office of the Press Secretary, "FACT SHEET: President Obama's SupplierPay Initiative Expands; 21 Additional Companies Pledge to Strengthen America's Small Businesses," *White House*, November 17, 2014, https://obamawhitehouse.archives.gov/the-press-office/2014/11/17/fact-sheet-president-obama-s-supplierpay-initiative-expands-21-additiona.

14. "English Summary," *Betaalme.nu*, Accessed June 29, 2017, https://www.betaalme.nu/paymenow.

15. Department for Business, Energy & Industrial Strategy, "Prompt Payment Code," *Chartered Institute of Credit Management*, Accessed June 29, 2017, http://www.promptpaymentcode.org.uk.

16. Bourree Lam, "Where Do Firms Go When They Die?," *The Atlantic*, April 12, 2015, https://www.theatlantic.com/business/archive/2015/04/where-do-firms-go-when-they-die/390249/.

17. Neil Perkins, "Is the Life Expectancy of Companies Really Shrinking?," *Only Dead Fish*, September 1, 2015, http://www.onlydeadfish.co.uk/only_dead_fish/2015/09/is-the-life-expectancy-of-companies-really-shrinking.html.

18. "Innosight," Accessed June 29, 2017, https://www.innosight.com/.

19. Richard Foster and Sarah Kaplan, *Creative Destruction: Why Companies That Are Built to Last Underperform the Market – And How to Successfully Transform Them* (New York: Currency Doubleday, 2001).

20. "Creative Destruction Whips through Corporate America," *Innosight*, February 2012, https://www.innosight.com/insight/creative-destruction-whips-through-corporate-america-an-innosight-executive-briefing-on-corporate-strategy/.

21. Alan Earls, "From Germany to the World: Industry 4.0," *Smart Industry*, April 20, 2015, https://www.smartindustry.com/blog/smart-industry-connect/from-germany-to-the-world-industry-4-0/.

22. "Elementum," Accessed June 29, 2017, http://www.elementum.com/.

23. "Gothenburg port strikes planned next week," *JOC.com*, February 17, 2017, http://www.joc.com/port-news/european-ports/gothenburg-port-strikes-planned-next-week_20170217.html.

17

Seizing the Opportunity

Magnus Lind and Kelly Barner

Customer-Centricity Creates Alignment and Eradicates Silos

One of the challenges facing the CFO is the need to make his or her office more streamlined and homogenous and to align the departments that comprise it. Everyone must share a common goal. How else can we eradicate silos, obtain process flow thinking, and make the CFO's office drive towards a common objective? Is there a more compelling and strategic objective than building profitable customer value over time?

In Appendix 1 we present the findings from a study conducted in early 2017, in which finance executives were asked to list how they expect the finance function to develop. The top three most selected 'predictions' were:

1. **Finance will work more cross-functionally**. This requires alignment along common objectives and targets and the eradication of silos.
2. **Finance will expand its remit to cover the whole supply chain** as a way to optimize the distribution of financial risk and capital, or leveraging an ecosystem play.
3. **Finance will participate in redesigns of the company's business model** to add revenue streams and/or become more competitive.

M. Lind
Skanor Group Ltd, London, UK

K. Barner
Buyers Meeting Point, Shrewsbury, MA, USA

© The Author(s) 2018
M. Lind, K. Barner, *Finance Unleashed*, DOI 10.1007/978-3-319-66370-8_17

Since the CFO's office consists of disparate functions (treasury, procurement, accounting, IT, etc), it often lacks a 'common language'. This requires alignment intra-company and inter-company in the ecosystem.

Allowing silos to build up is a management failure, unless it is intentional of course. Silos are the result of a disconnect between the overall objectives and targets of the company and what each individual function is doing. It often leads to an overemphasis of departmental importance, the formation of multiple departmental cultures, and – in the worst case – an 'us v. them' rivalry. A silo mentality is further emphasized when targets and objectives are chopped up into intermittent, disjointed, departmental targets that add up to a divergent (and sometimes contradictory) company-wide way of working.

This is why customer-centric targets and objectives are so powerful. They unite the company and enable cooperation across the ecosystem by focusing on increasing the satisfaction of current and future end-customers. Customer satisfaction becomes the common denominator for the CFO's office, the company, and the end-to-end supply chain. A customer-centric view is therefore natural when approaching the financial supply chain.

How is it possible to achieve this? Lean Six Sigma recommends listening to the 'Voice of the Customer' (VOC)[1] to facilitate interactions with customers and understand their drivers, needs, and wants.

Four common ways of accessing the VOC are:

1. **Conduct interviews** directly with the customers, the customer's customers, and distributors. The results will be a direct effect of how you ask the questions and should therefore not be expected to provide more than a shallow understanding of why the customers buy from you and what they really want if you don't dig deep enough.
2. **Point-of-use observation**, where you make an effort to truly understand how customers use your product or service. This approach is similar to Clayton Christensen's "job-to-be-done".[2]
3. **Focus groups**, which are a form of less time-consuming interviews, provide multiple customer perspectives in a compressed format.
4. **Surveys**, which provide guidance and can confirm theories or expectations. Surveys can also measure customer satisfaction levels over time.

The above four, while recognized practices, are unlikely to be chosen by the CFO to expand his or her understanding of the customer. Meeting with peer groups, on the other hand, offers them an opportunity to learn more about the VOC in a way that leverages their current C-level role. This is one way for the CFO to lead by example and become an authority on customer-centricity.

A peer group is a way to regularly engage with customers in the B2B and B2G segments over a period of time (typically between two and five times a year). The purpose is not to discuss products and services, but to build up rapport with key customers and understand their evolving wants and needs. Together with their customers' CFOs (and treasurers, procurement, etc.), your company's finance leaders can share and discuss an agenda with the purpose of developing mutual value.

Running a peer group requires time and dedication and may justify the engagement of a professional moderator that holds the meetings together, does research, prepares the agenda, and shares results over time. When dealing with customers it is important to add value and avoid direct solicitation, both of which may lead to poor attendance and can even be counterproductive. The peer group should sincerely intend to benefit customers (and the hosting company, indirectly) by taking their input to heart so that it is possible to become better professionals and improve corporate performance. A peer group is not where you sell, it is where you gather intelligence and deepen your understanding of how customers reason and make decisions. Ambitious peer groups may even include external speakers to inspire and challenge the group. With time, these groups tend to become close knit, requiring a rigorous selection processes when inviting new members.

Each meeting can be as long as two days; however, few executives can stay away from their office for so long. Focused dinner or breakfast meetings work well too. The length and ambition of the meetings depends on if they are local or international, and whether they require travel. A good group size is 7–15 peers to allow for everyone to actively participate in the discussion.

Structure and Technology: Leveraging Transparency and Trust in an Ecosystem Play

Finance is based on trust, and notions of trust are rapidly changing. In the modern, global, virtually networked economy, trust is built between individuals and in communities using a third party to validate identities and facilitate interactions. Increased connectivity and trust open up new opportunities for cooperation over the financial supply chain, outside of the direct control and oversight of the banks. Working directly, company to company, enables us to transact more transparently and makes it easier to detect the inefficient use or allocation of capital and risk.

Think of your suppliers as outsourced production and your distributors as your interface and eyes to the market. Is your success based on an 'ecosystem play' or is it restricted to how your company performs in isolation? Transparency is the central component that future (financial) supply chain systems will provide throughout the whole chain. Many finance operations now take a link versus a chain perspective. They regard each company in the supply chain as independent of its ecosystem instead of being a fully ingrained part of it. This is also true for financial IT systems that have been developed from the perspective of automating and mimicking manual financial processes, one independent link at a time, in isolation. Few resource planning systems have disrupted the way we work; they have primarily automated and optimized legacy (physical supply chain) processes. In the future, it is the financial systems that will disrupt how we work. Those that will be the most successful will start by understanding the job-to-be-done for the customer and focus on progress, not process. They will also provide transparency over the whole chain, allowing the community to carry out trusted transactions.

Cooperation over the whole chain requires that each link (or entity) trust one another. Up to this point, trust in the financial system has been dependent on legislation, regulation, legacy institutions, and belief. Just because a US dollar bill states it is legal tender doesn't mean it will always be worth more than the paper it is printed on. We are taught to believe that the government (with the help of the central bank) will always be able to honor their debt. This belief system is based on rigorous governance and, frankly, broad-scale manipulation of perspectives. Just because a central bank can print money doesn't mean the money is worth anything. It may be a legal tender of nothing. But we all want to believe it stands for something because it is a good system (when it works) and we depend on it to live our lives in the way we do.

If the system doesn't work, and the trust is broken, we are left to live with a system such as we see in Zimbabwe or Venezuela, with over-inflated currencies that do not provide a store of value over time. Renaming the currency or printing more money doesn't suffice when trust in the currency has been lost because regaining people's trust takes a very long time. Central banks and governments are therefore persistent in ensuring that their policies and regulations will provide financial stability. They don't want people to lose that trust. This legacy system of trust is built on institutions to which we are connected as individuals and the institutions validate each individual to each other.

Trust in the Internet is a key factor changing legacy concepts of trust in the financial system. It is a fact little discussed, but central to the disruptions we are currently experiencing.

During the recent crisis, there were times that made owning Bitcoin look safer than storing your life savings in a Greek bank. Bitcoin is stored in an ecosystem, outside of and without control by any government or institution. Its value cannot be corrupted through increasing the amount of Bitcoin in circulation (as any central bank currency can risk corruption by printing too much of it). The supply of Bitcoin is predetermined and therefore it is protected against hyperinflation. In times of financial uncertainty, it can provide a unique form of safe haven.

On the other hand, price fluctuations to other currencies and lack of government control and regulation limit the likelihood that Bitcoin will become a widely accepted means of payment or store of value. Even though Bitcoin, or any other non-regulated means of payment for that matter, is only one example of how the concept of trust has changed, the introduction of Bitcoin in November of 2008[3] was a form of revolt against the central banking model that, in the opinion of some, had stopped benefiting the people. The founders of Bitcoin believed the institutions were corrupted and not trustworthy.

'New' Trust Relies on the Ecosystem

New trust is distributed and centralized at the same time. It is based on the ecosystem and on machines and it complements traditional institutional trust.

Imagine you travel to Helsinki and you need somewhere to sleep for the night. You try to book a room on location, even though it is late in the afternoon and you are in a residential area with very few people walking the streets and no hotels. You are a male in your 50s and you spot a young, single mother just entering one of the buildings. You take a chance and approach her, saying, "Hi there, I'm John. Can I stay in your spare bed for one night please? I will be glad to pay you of course." She will most likely rush into the building, secure the door, lock you out, and disappear. In the worst case, she will call the police to report a crazy guy in her neighborhood.

As an alternative, consider what would have happened if she had accepted the offer. Would John have dared to go through with the arrangement? Would it be safe for him? Who would be waiting for him in the apartment? How likely is it that they would achieve mutual trust?

This precise thing happens, thousands of times every day all the world over. People let strangers into their homes and allow them to sleep over. People enter the home of complete strangers to get a night's sleep. Both sides of the transaction trust Airbnb to protect them and to take care of the financials. Airbnb is a central machine managing a distributed community. It is not a government, nor is it an institution. Airbnb isn't even regulated (except as a private enterprise of course). And yet Airbnb allows the man and the single mother to transact safely, to ensure governance, and to achieve trust. In fact, John had no need to worry and he had a safe night's sleep, without worrying about being robbed or killed. The single mother didn't need to worry either.

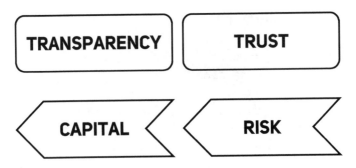

Fig. 17.1 Transparency, trust, capital, and risk. The four core components to be covered by modern IT solutions in the financial supply chain

They both trusted the machine and the reviews and endorsements it provided from people neither of them knew – the ecosystem. The payment transaction was safely conducted on Airbnb's trusted server. This is a new type of trust, one that is very important, especially since trust is the foundation of any financial system. This kind of trust doesn't (only) depend on traditional institutions.

No financial system can operate without mutual trust. What does that mean for future technical solutions? How can we use this realization to improve the competitiveness of our supply chains? How can we use machines to develop and maintain the trust of everyone in the ecosystem? Future trust will be based on our position in the ecosystem.

A strong supply chain is transparent and provides its players with the trust for distributing capital optimally. In this book, we accuse narrow-minded capital metrics of increasing the risk of supply chain disruption or a loss of corporate competitive advantage. With transparency and trust, we can distribute capital (and reduce the need for some of it) more optimally over the chain, reducing the risk of disruption, costs, and tied-up capital. Through an ecosystem play, we can decrease the total use of capital and the associated risks and costs, benefitting the customer and our competitiveness.

This is also true of financial risk (e.g., credit, foreign exchange, commodity price, and interest rate risks). Imagine an auto manufacturer receiving and assembling components from their suppliers. A car contains a lot of commodities (aluminum, copper, steel, etc.) and yet it is not the auto manufacturer that bears the direct price risks. Instead it is spread out over their suppliers who need to add economic buffers to cover for adverse price movements. Those buffers add up over the whole chain and add extra costs for the end-customer. A better solution would be to handle the risks at each source from the perspective of one combined chain instead of acting as many independent links, loosely interconnected.

IT solutions for modern financial supply chains will cover and support transparency, trust, capital allocation, and risk management. They will act in real time and focus on the objectives your customer is trying to achieve with the products and/or services they buy from your ecosystem. They allow the organizations to strive for continuous progress, not just automate legacy processes. They build systems around the financial supply chain rather than just the physical supply chain.

Providing transparency is critical when developing or choosing software for the financial supply chain. Transparency is paramount, not only in your company's confined part of the supply chain, but over the whole chain. Modern systems will be real-time, take into account all important parameters, and function unrestricted by the borders of legal entities. Modern systems will act like a navigation system in a car; if you get off-course they will recalculate the route for you automatically. This means Industry 4.0 will also encompass the financial supply chain.

With this background, we must ask ourselves if the IT solutions for the financial supply chain will build on the fragmentation brought to us by fintech or if we will see the huge, functionality-ridden solutions already available on the market extended to include even more bells and whistles? Will we continue to be confined to systems that take a one-company view or will solutions evolve to present us with an 'ecosystem play' model? What components should we consider? What solutions do you need to give your customer what they really want?

We could be guided by what is happening in the physical chain, where transparency is quickly becoming paramount in Industry 4.0. Companies want to know where each bolt and nut, each unit of freight, each truck, and each finished product is in the chain at any given moment. We want to have access to that information in real time and in a format that allows us to conduct an analysis of trends over time – not analysis for its own sake, but to support us in our mission of providing valuable services and solutions to our customers. When will we know where each £, $, €, etc. is, and how they flow – in real-time?

An interesting observation is that the treasurer often sits at the center of this financial IT transformation because he or she is managing bank and fintech provider relationships. The treasurer is also in control of the cash flow and cash forecasting, which may be the starting point of unravelling the financial supply chain. How will the role of the treasurer evolve and how can treasury infrastructure better support the whole company, or even the whole ecosystem?

Look for New Solutions

Many of the current solutions are built around the flow of the physical supply chain. Financial transactions are treated as a residual and are managed in an intermittent flow. In the 2008 financial crisis, a corporation's cash flow became so much more important than before the crisis when cash was available in abundance. This is what always happens in economic liquidity crises, since debt expansion cannot continue forever.[4]

Since the financial crisis, the boat has rocked more often than usual for the CFO. As a consequence, we can now develop new models to transact financially, making flows less intermittent and more based on the ecosystem play and peer-to-peer in lieu of what an old-fashioned bank/correspondent banking network allowed (so far). The 2008 crisis was not just an ordinary financial liquidity crisis waiting for 'recovery' debt to start to expand again. In 2008, a large technological change happened at the same time. Blockchain,[5] more broadly labeled as Distributed Ledger Technology (DLT), was introduced. If that wasn't enough, the Bank of International Settlements (or BIS, the central bank of central banks, based in Basel and a financial regulator) led the push to further dis-intermediate banks towards non-financial corporations with new versions of the so-called 'Basel regulation'. All of this was taking place while the global economy moved to a service and information based, rather than manufacturing based, economy.

It bears repeating that the treasury department is central here, as it is the CFOs' and the CEOs' contact point to the banks and to new solutions, delivered by fintech and other vendors. We would therefore say that the treasurer could theoretically be your company's financial supply chain coordinator. A coordinator will be important since many of the new IT solutions naturally bridge current silos in the CFO's office and the implementation requires shared responsibilities and agendas from at least two departments. Without a silo-bridging coordinator you face the risk of losing the battle of resources to more highly prioritized silo activities (see Appendix 2).

The development of DLT is exponentially fast, as is the number of possible applications. The DLT is not a technological revolution per se, but it is a new way of applying existing technology to finance. The DLT transactions are conducted directly between buyer and seller, a huge change from how we have transacted financially in the past. That is why it is forcefully disrupting not only banks, but also corporations. DLT will disrupt the whole financial system.

In February 2017, the BIS issued an analytical framework: Distributed Ledger Technology in Payment, Clearing and Settlement.[6,7] The initial resistance against so-called cryptocurrencies by regulators and central banks when Bitcoin was originally released has definitely changed: they are now supporters of DLT, if not of Bitcoin and other cryptocurrencies. There are numerous examples of this, for instance from the ECB,[8] the Federal Reserve,[9] and the Monetary Authority of Singapore,[10] all of whom have started to find DLT application areas for themselves.

One of the first ideas for how a central bank could use DLT was launched by uber-smart J.P. Koning on his blog in October 2014.[11] Koning presented 'FedCoins', a central bank currency transacted on a DLT managed by the Federal Reserve and replacing USD bills and coins in circulation. The Federal Reserve openly engaged in a discussion on J.P. Koning's idea almost immediately since FedCoin would introduce many advantages to the current coins and bills regime.[12]

FedCoin would be issued at par with the USD (meaning that 1 FedCoin equals 1 USD). Currency pegs usually don't work since they are unilateral and thereby build up imbalances that sooner or later lead to the peg falling (compare the recent CHF/EUR debacle in 2015[13]). In this case, however, it would be the Fed issuing both the FedCoin and the USD making this peg credible over the long term. The FedCoin/USD peg takes away the volatility inherent in the price of a cryptocurrency. FedCoins should not replace the USD per se, only the USD bills and coins. This would increase traceability, ensuring effective anti-money laundering and hindering tax evasion. FedCoins are electronic and therefore much cheaper to maintain than physical bills and coins, and since FedCoins replace bills and coins they would not have any interest rate. The commercial banks and credit unions would manage the accounts for FedCoin for the holders. All transactions would take place over the central bank DLT where the current financial institutions act as verifiers of each transaction. FedCoin could be used for all cash transactions using a mobile phone or any other device.

Other benefits include:

- FedCoin would be an added monetary tool for the central banks. They could choose to issue Fedcoins or USD and they would gain a better estimate of the money supply since it is practically impossible to keep track of physical bills and coins in circulation.
- The economy would benefit from this low-cost real-time payment system far away from the current archaic, expensive, slow, and cumbersome systems of bills and coins.
- Fedcoin would also reduce systemic fraud caused by credit cards and fake bills.

The DLT has the potential to be nothing short of revolutionary for the financial system. Other areas and examples where the DLT is being applied:

Trade Finance IBM has built a DLT solution for a Chinese company, allowing them to better track goods as they are shipped and delivered, encrypt documentation, and provide open access to the transaction record, facilitating faster transaction authentication.[14]

Another recent trade finance example is a cooperation between Deutsche Bank, HSBC, KBC, Natixis, Rabobank, Société Générale, and UniCredit to develop a new product called Digital Trade Chain (DTC). DTC is based on a prototype trade finance tool developed by Belgian bank KBC. Using DLT connects trade parties – buyers, sellers, transporters, banks – financing the deals on either side.[15]

Identity Confirming identity is the basis of trust. You need to know you are dealing with the right person.[16] DLT is perfect for this application, which is yet unsolved as proven by the estimated US$20 billion credit card fraud per annum as of 2015.[17]

DLT is also expected to make Anti-Money-Laundering (AML) and Know-Your-Customer (KYC) processes more efficient. The DLT might therefore decrease the hassle of opening a foreign bank account for instance.[18]

Payments This is the original area where Blockchain was applied, the mother of the DLT. We can highlight Ripple[19] which is building a global infrastructure for bank payments, and SWIFT,[20] the incumbent bank payment processor, who has entered into this space. Think about what it would mean if DLT did for payments what Skype has done for telecom.

Securities Settlement, Clearing, and Issuance In December 2015, NASDAQ introduced 'NASDAQ Linq',[21] based on a DLT, enabling share issuers to issue new shares with far shorter settlement times and less use of paper. NASDAQ Linq has developed since its initial launch and has added DLT based payment capabilities.[22]

Insurance DLT disruption in the insurance market builds partly on new trust models and how DLT can facilitate entering into so-called 'smart contracts'.[23] The aim is to broaden what can be insured, introduce new parties, and create more transparent pricing mechanics, (hopefully) leading to lower fees.

There are even more revolutionary applications popping up from the DLT technology. Consider the ICO (Initial Coin Offering),[24] which is raising capital through issuing a token, or your own cryptocoins that can be exchanged for cryptocurrencies, convertible to fiat currencies ($, €, £ etc). It is an alternative to issuing shares. There are multiple ways to structure it, and a simple form is that the founders keep a small number of the tokens; for example, a foundation keeps say 40 per cent and the rest of the tokens are issued to those that provide services and value to the company, for instance as open-sourced code or techniques. Imagine if Facebook (NASDAQ: FB) issued tokens to its two billion member user base for the relative value of their content (e.g. number of clicks and shares) making them benefit if the tokens increase in value. After all, it is the content providers who make the user value of Facebook.[25] It is an interesting concept that can turn current wealth structures upside down. Although the ICO is gaining steam, we need to consider that it is still an unregulated ocean where fraudsters may swim. And yet it serves as an example of how the DLT has the potential to dramatically disrupt the current financial system, which underpins the power structures of our times.

Getting from Here to There

A CFO may need someone who measures and leads financial supply chain improvements – a financial supply chain coordinator. This role is similar to a physical supply chain coordinator and should have (or obtain) a level of expertise in finance and Lean Six Sigma, with a lateral and fairly senior approach to business. The financial supply chain coordinator will make recommendations for improvement of productivity, quality, efficiency of operations, and customer value generation. He or she will also be the point of contact to vendors of financial supply chain solutions, establish a common language in the CFO's office, and liaise with the ecosystem through departmental managers. Of course, the financial supply chain coordinator should also have a customer-centric mindset.

CFOs who learn from their supply chain ecosystem will find ways to:

- Streamline cash flows over the supply (and demand) chain by examining trade finance practices and opportunities to decrease waste in the form of float, tied-up cash, and fees.
- Measure and participate in reducing working capital over the whole supply chain, lowering costs and improving the funding of supplier innovation capabilities.
- Measure the cost of (non-interest) finance in the supply chain, including banking costs and trade finance expenses and look for ways to reduce them.
- Extract the cost of finance from product/service price to make it visible. Clarify what customers are really paying for. Do you pay suppliers to take on expensive debt costs, camouflaged as cost of goods?

- Perform a post-mortem analysis of each supply chain disruption. Determine if disruptions could have been avoided with better capital allocation or other financial measures. Articulate how customers have been affected by the disruption.
- Reduce the number of payments and foreign exchange in the supply chain.
- Measure the supply chain's contribution to (financial) innovation.[26]
- Measure and manage customer and supplier credit risk and default rates.

Innovation by the CFO

Traditionally, the role of the CFO has included protecting the balance sheet, safeguarding governance, and bringing order to the chaos created by volatile markets, changes in customer demand, and constant adaptations of the business. Innovation has been restricted to the physical chain of goods and services and largely allowed the financial system to remain the same over time (albeit with incremental improvements). All this changed in 2008 with the disruption of finance through a combination of deep financial crisis, introduction of new technology and regulations, and the evolution of fintech, which brings vast opportunities for new, improved business models in non-financial companies. It allows finance executives to transform the finance role from an expert role to a more lateral business leader role. It is an exciting time to be in finance.

It is not only the banking sector that is being affected by the disruption in finance. The corporate sector is involved as well. In fact, it may well be that the corporate sector will be disrupted even more than the banks since they currently own the physical supply chain. If the financial supply chain merges with the physical one, it will naturally make corporates into distributors of financial services to their customers.

If corporations plan to supply financial services to their customers (and suppliers), they will have to get support from the banks, other financial institutions, and fintech suppliers. Refer to the UPS and DHL example in Chapter 11, where they deliver financial services to their customers. They use the banks for funding and have fintech vendors supply the portals, which are often white labeled. Apple, Facebook, and Amazon et al. are also adding financial services as separate offerings. UPS and DHL strengthen their logistics offerings by adding financial services, and thus increase the competitiveness of their core business. This approach exemplifies the changing role of finance. They have opened whole new revenue streams – even new markets – while safeguarding the company's competitiveness and extending its lifespan.

Innovation, especially disruptive innovation, is now a main threat to incumbent companies. This is exacerbated by the fact that they don't usually have the best capacity for innovative disruption to begin with. In Clayton Christensen's classic *The Innovator's Dilemma*[27] this problem is exquisitely described and analyzed in full. Most big companies do not have the DNA to foster disruptive innovation – not because of poor management, but just because the management and company are excellent on incremental innovation and the operations are organized and optimized for it. The consequence is that successful and well-managed companies could very well kill disruptive innovation. Christensen concludes that for disruptive innovation to have the highest probability of success, it should happen outside of the big company structure and potentially even be allowed to kill its own legacy products over time (which is a far better option than having someone else do the killing). Compare Murat Erden's reasoning in Chapter 7 to allow innovation to disrupt the current organization and connect innovation directly to the board and have it run independent of the current executive leadership (who can act threatened).

In *The Innovator's Dilemma*, Christensen takes the example of how personal computers killed the minicomputer industry by initially offering inferior functionality to a less sophisticated market with less buying power at a lower price. Over time, the personal computer used its potential to offer superior product features at a much more competitive price using consistent standards. The PC went from a questionable beginning to effectively eradicating the minicomputer industry.

Innovation: The Center of the Finance Function

Finance (including the functions of treasury, controlling, accounting, IT, procurement, supply chain, etc.) has suddenly become so much more than it ever was in the past. It requires a new leadership style and correspondingly altered performance metrics.

The tendency for disruptive innovation to start at younger, nimbler companies creates a dependency on the part of larger companies. These innovative companies could be your suppliers – the ones that are suffering under the heavy weight of costly capital and maybe even volatile fluctuations of currencies and commodities. The price of pushing working capital up and down the supply chain can be very high in the medium to long term. Not only does it increase the risk of financial vulnerability and supply chain disruption, it may also reduce the chain's capacity for innovation.

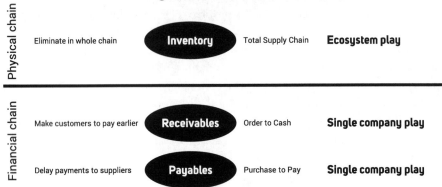

Fig. 17.2 This figure presents the singularity of the approaches of rationalization of the physical versus the financial supply chain (The idea behind this figure comes from a handbook on working capital management)

In fact, it has become increasingly apparent that accounting is not a good measure of the state of business at all. Accounting does not always take a holistic perspective (and is not customer-centric), and in the end we risk steering our company to comply with the very accounting principles that jeopardize our competitiveness and agility. Interestingly, on October 12, 2016, Mark Weinberger, the Global Chairman and CEO of EY shared an update on LinkedIn:

> Did you know? In 1975, 83% of the average firm's value was counted on the balance sheet. Today, it is only 16%. Quarterly reports just don't capture most of a company's true, long-term value. And, as result, they push companies to focus on short-term value over long-term investment. We need to overcome this and find a new, standardized way of reporting the full value of a company beyond the basic financials. #InclusiveCapitalism[28]

So true.

We cannot rely on accounting reports to provide us with the insight and intelligence for the financial supply chain. As if this wasn't enough, Charlie Bean explains to us in Chapter 12 that not even national statistics (such as GDP and inflation) are adjusted to this new world. So, this larger context provides an illustration of the extent of the ongoing financial and economic disruption.

Imagine if you assigned one person in finance as responsible for innovation and they reported directly to the CFO, perhaps with a dotted line to the group innovation director. The purpose of the role would be to find ways to disrupt how finance operations are run today. He or she could be responsible for coordinating the financial supply chain, or the innovator could be the CFO, or there might be a Wealth Creator in the company (as described in Chapter 9). If an innovator is to disrupt, they must have free hands and understand customer needs and wants, preferably before the customer.

An innovator will threaten the status quo and therefore will require the full support of the leadership team in all situations since conflicts of interest (hidden or open) will occur. If conflicts do not arise, the innovator has not performed. You need to set up criteria for the success of innovation and predetermine when and how to pull the plug of failed innovations (or a better word: 'learnings'). Productivity can be increased if the whole CFO's office is introduced to 'design thinking' techniques so the innovator doesn't become isolated, working alone in a black box that no one understands (and fears). We highlight the importance of alignment and having everyone contribute. Innovation is inclusive, not exclusive.

Developments are taking place so fast that keeping a close eye on them is paramount. The CFO is heading one of the fastest-moving areas of all. The context is constantly changing and that is what Singularity University,[29] co-founded by Ray Kurzweil and Peter Diamandis, is focused on. Singularity University is based in California and has as its mission to "educate, inspire, and empower leaders to apply exponential technologies to address humanity's grand challenges". They build on the realization that Gordon Moore's law (the observation that the number of transistors in a dense integrated circuit doubles approximately every two years), is more generally valid. In the "Law of Accelerating Returns",[30] Ray Kurzweil claims that all technological change is exponential, not linear as the human brain is programmed to understand. Developments do not happen in steps of one. Instead, performance over price doubles every 12–18 months. This means if you blink, you may miss it.

Many mature and well-run companies, sometimes with tens of thousands of employees and market capitalizations in the tens of billions USD, are run with a linear strategy. Meanwhile, an entrepreneur can find ways to replace what you are doing with a much nimbler, cheaper, and more attractive offering than the established competition. Your current assets, like a large sales force or a well-established brand, can lose their value practically overnight.

In "*Exponential Organizations*" by Salim Ismail, Yuri van Geest and Michael Malone,[31] (a book we *highly* recommend that everyone read) we learn how new organizations can be 10x better, faster, and cheaper than established companies, and how to compete successfully with them. They talk about adaptability and flexibility (remember Darwin), lean start-up techniques, etc. To prove the point, they take the example of the exponential development of the performance of price relations predicting that in 25 years all energy could be delivered by solar techniques only.[32]

How will thinking exponentially change your value proposition?

Good Examples

Finance executives can become effective business people positioned to drive the future of their company and industry. There are several excellent examples in this book that present what is possible, for instance the UPS and DHL business case in Chapter 11 and the transformation of Turkcell presented below.

UPS and DHL have demonstrated how the financial and physical chains can merge to create greater customer value. They took the opportunity to develop a convenient set of financial products they could bundle and offer together with their logistics products. This decision dramatically increased their competitiveness and now drives profitability improvements, expanded customer relationships, and growth of the customer base. UPS and DHL moved from offering an easily replaceable commodity to becoming business-critical partners to their customers. They use IT solutions from fintech companies for supplier and invoice financing and they ensure funding and credit risk management through banks as well as non-bank financiers. They then brand the whole solution in their own name and bundle it together with their better-known logistics solutions. This is one example of a financial solution developed from the vantage point of the customer. UPS and DHL have managed to engage several stakeholders in their ecosystem around one effort and strive to increase their reach – and therefore brand 'stickiness' – deeper into the supply chains of their customers. This is a perfect example of an 'ecosystem play'; UPS and DHL have found a way to improve customer value in a fashion few customers predicted.

Turkcell (BİST: TCELL, NYSE: TKC) is another example of how financial products can be used to transform businesses. Turkcell added the services of a consumer finance company to boost its revenues. Turkcell is the leading mobile phone operator in Turkey, headquartered in Istanbul. The company has approximately 35 million subscribers and introduced a radical business transformation in 2016 with the effort to launch a consumer finance company to offer financial products to its customer base.

Turkcell had accepted the golden days of the traditional GSM model were over with the looming shift to a services-focused world. Merely owning and charging for a telecommunications infrastructure could not be expected to support them going forward the way it had done in the past.

Turkcell had been financing the devices as a by-product and decided to build on it and provide financial support for technology in all aspects of life. In the financing business, Turkcell had developed an exceptional competence in managing a very large credit portfolio for its subscriber base, some of whom even are 'unbanked' (i.e., not having a bank account and managing all financial transactions in cash and without an official credit history). Turkcell expanded its mission by adding a finance company operating in the area of fintech, (where finance meets technology) serving financial needs to individuals and corporate entities. New innovations will be released by Turkcell through this new company. The goal has become to provide financial support for technology in all aspects of life, and this will also serve Turkcell's digital journey.

The plan devised by Turkcell was as smart as it was bold. To keep customers loyal to the Turkcell network, they needed to have the fastest and most reliable network. The return on investment would be ensured not only by increasing raw data consumption, but through adoption of Turkcell's own mobile apps and solutions. In the spring of 2016, they rolled out one of the fastest mobile networks in the world, based on 4.5G, reaching up to 300 Mbit/sec in the largest cities.[33] Meanwhile, they launched the consumer finance company Turkcell Finansman A.S.,[34] under the brand 'Financell', to offer several financial products to their subscription base. Turkcell leveraged its strength of having the devices and a distributor network in the hands of 35 million people. Try to imagine how difficult it would be for anyone to compete with a finance network consisting of 35 million branches. By the end of 2016, Financell had exceeded the financial forecasts made at the time of its launch.

By the end of the first quarter of 2017, Financell reached approximately 3 billion Lira in loans and 2.5 million customers, which is a big achievement in a very short time frame. Turkcell's smartphone penetration in Turkey continued to rise on the back of this financing boost, reaching 68 percent at the end of the first quarter of 2017, which is a 13 percent increase compared to one year earlier. In addition, average mobile usage has increased 69 percent to 3 GB per user, which gives a fresh impetus to the company's financial results.

We have described several ways and methods by which CFOs can leverage opportunities in the financial supply chain. We have raised the bar by focusing on the exponential development of new technologies and the power of for example 1, 2, 4, 8, 16… (or 2, 4, 16, 256…) instead of the linear development we are used to and better can grasp; 1, 2, 3, 4, 5…

If that isn't inspiring enough for you, consider the "Fear of Becoming Irrelevant" (or FOBI). If nothing else, the FOBI will prove to be a very powerful driver for CFOs in the process of transforming from a 'command and control' role to becoming the center of the company's business innovation. There comes a time when business as usual is the biggest risk, and customer-facing financial solutions may provide the remedy.

We leave you with a quote by Ray Kurzweil (co-founder of the Singularity University): "I realize that most inventions fail not because the R&D department can't get them to work, but because the timing is wrong – not all of the enabling factors are at play where they are needed. Inventing is a lot like surfing: you have to anticipate and catch the wave at just the right moment."[35] For the financial supply chain the wave is building up.

Notes

1. Michael L. George, David Rowlands, Mark Price, and John Maxley, *The Lean Six Sigma Pocket Toolbook: A Quick Reference Guide to 100 Tools for Improving Quality and Speed* (New York: McGraw-Hill, 2005).
2. Clayton M. Christensen, Taddy Hall, Karen Dillon, David S. Duncan, *Competing Against Luck* (New York: HarperBusiness, 2016), p. xiv.
3. Satoshi Nakamoto, "Original Satoshi Nakamoto Bitcoin White Paper," *BlockStreet*, posted by James Evans on August 11, 2015, https://blockstreet.info/news/2015-08-11/original-satoshi-nakamoto-bitcoin-white-paper-32769.
4. Reinhart, Carmen M. and Kenneth S. Rogoff, *This Time Is Different: Eight Centuries of Financial Folly* (Princeton, New Jersey: Princeton University Press, 2009).
5. McConaghy, Trent "Blockchain Infrastructure Landscape: A First Principles Framing," https://blog.bigchaindb.com/blockchain-infrastructure-landscape-a-first-principles-framing-92cc5549bafe
6. Committee on Payments and Market Infrastructures, "Distributed Ledger Technology in Payment, Clearing and Settlement: an Analytical Framework," *Bank for International Settlements*, February 2017, https://www.bis.org/cpmi/publ/d157.pdf.
7. You will find a good analysis of the BIS analytics framework here: Chris Skinner, "BIS Endorse [sic] Distributed Ledger Technology (DLT) for Payments Clearing and Settlement," *Chris Skinner's Blog*, March 2017, https://thefinanser.com/2017/03/bis-endorse-distributed-ledger-technology-dlt-payments-clearing-settlement.html/.

8. Yves Mersch, "Distributed Ledger Technology: Role and Relevance of the ECB," *European Central Bank*, December 6, 2016, https://www.ecb.europa.eu/press/key/date/2016/html/sp161206.en.html.

9. Jerome H. Powell, "Innovation, Technology, and the Payments System," *Federal Reserve*, March 3, 2017, https://www.federalreserve.gov/newsevents/speech/powell20170303a.htm.

10. Jordan Daniell, "Singapore's Central Bank Concludes Distributed Ledger Trial," *ETHNews.com*, May 31, 2017, https://www.ethnews.com/singapores-central-bank-concludes-distributed-ledger-trial.

11. J.P. Koning, "Fedcoin," *Moneyness*, October 19, 2014, http://jpkoning.blogspot.se/2014/10/fedcoin.html.

12. Magnus Lind, "Did you know the Templar Knights developed the current payment system?" *LinkedIn Publishing*, May 17, 2015, https://www.linkedin.com/pulse/did-you-know-templar-knights-developed-current-payment-magnus-lind.

13. C.W., "Why the Swiss unpegged the franc," *The Economist*, January 18, 2015, http://www.economist.com/blogs/economist-explains/2015/01/economist-explains-13.

14. BI Intelligence, "IBM is Going All In on Blockchain for Trade Finance," *Business Insider*, April 12, 2017, http://www.businessinsider.com/ibm-is-going-all-in-on-blockchain-for-trade-finance-2017-4?r=US&IR=T&IR=T.

15. Oscar Williams-Grut, "Deutsche Bank, HSBC, and Five Other Big Banks are Collaborating on a Blockchain Project," *Business Insider*, January 16, 2017, http://www.businessinsider.com/deutsche-bank-hsbc-kbc-natixis-rabobank-socit-gnrale-and-unicredit-work-on-digital-trade-chain-dtc-2017-1.

16. Jonathan Chester, "How the Blockchain Will Secure Your Online Identity," *Forbes*, March 3, 2017, https://www.forbes.com/sites/jonathanchester/2017/03/03/how-the-blockchain-will-secure-your-online-identity/#7749df855523.

17. "The Nilson Report," Accessed July 1, 2017, https://www.nilsonreport.com/.

18. Matthew Britton, "Could Blockchain Solve the KYC/AML Challenge?," *BCS Consulting*, September 29, 2016, https://www.bcsconsulting.com/blog/new-technology-can-enable-human-bank/.

19. "Ripple," Accessed July 1, 2017, https://ripple.com/.

20. Swift, Accessed July 1, 2017, https://www.swift.com/.

21. Nasdaq, Will Briganti, *Nasdaq Linq Enables First-Ever Private Securities Issuance Documented with Blockchain Technology*, December 30, 2015, http://ir.nasdaq.com/releasedetail.cfm?releaseid=948326.

22. Tom Groenfeldt, "Blockchain Moves Ahead with Nasdaq-Citi Platform, Hyperledger and Ethereum," *Forbes*, May 22, 2017, https://www.forbes.com/sites/tomgroenfeldt/2017/05/22/blockchain-moves-ahead-with-nasdaq-citi-platform-hyperledger-and-ethereum-growth/#3a07ef6b7333.

23. "Smart Contracts Explained: The Ultimate Guide to Understanding Blockchain Smart Contracts," Accessed July 1, 2017, http://www.block-chaintechnologies.com/blockchain-smart-contracts.

24. Alex Wilhelm, "WTF is an ICO?" Techcrunch, May 23, 2017, https://tech-crunch.com/2017/05/23/wtf-is-an-ico/.

25. Trent McConaghy, "Tokenize the Enterprise … And Melt It Into the Community. Rinse, Repeat." BigChainDB, June 6, 2017, https://blog.bigchaindb.com/tokenize-the-enterprise-23d51bafb536.

26. Pierre Rougier, "9 Best Practices to Boost Supplier Innovation," *Kepler*, November 29, 2016, http://www.kepler-consulting.com/en/9-best-practices-boost-supplier-innovation/.

27. Clayton Christensen, *The Innovator's Dilemma: When New Technologies Cause Great Firms to Fail* (Boston: Harvard Business Review Press, 1997).

28. Mark Weinberger, Twitter post, October 10, 2016, 10:52 a.m, https://twitter.com/Mark_Weinberger/status/785493118607122432.

29. https://su.org/

30. Ray Kurzwell, "The Law of Accelerating Returns," *Kurzwell*, March 7, 2001, http://www.kurzweilai.net/the-law-of-accelerating-returns.

31. "Exponential Organizations," Accessed July 1, 2017, http://exponentialorgs.com/.

32. Salim Ismail, "Top 10 Exponential Companies," *CNBC* Video, 3:28, June 3, 2015, http://video.cnbc.com/gallery/?video=3000385249&play=1.

33. Turkcell, Hande Asik, *The Fastest of the Fastest: Turkcell Officially Launches 4.5G in Turkey*, April 1, 2016, http://www.businesswire.com/news/home/20160401005226/en/Fastest-Fastest-Turkcell-Officially-Launches-4.5G-Turkey.

34. "Turkcell Finansman," Accessed July 1, 2017, https://www.bloomberg.com/profiles/companies/1476016D:TI-turkcell-finansman-as.

35. Dr. Luis M. Proenza, "The Future Ain't What It Used to Be (2013 Spring Commencement Ceremony Sunday Afternoon)," *WayBack Machine*, May 12, 2013, https://web.archive.org/web/20140419011924/https://www.uakron.edu/president/speeches_statements/?id=c6856afc-067b-40d5-bfc1-ac93f118e3f5.

18

Finance Unleashed: A Practical Model

Magnus Lind and Kelly Barner

In this chapter, we provide you with a practical model for implementing customer-centricity, supply chain process thinking, and innovation agility. It is a model for getting you from here to there and to assist executive teams and boards (with an emphasis on the CFO) with the redesign and refocus of finance. The model has three primary components or phases:

1. Customer-centric – Listen & Map
2. Process – Structure & Technology
3. Innovation – Create & Measure

Customer-Centric Targets and Objectives for the CFO

Add value to the demand side of the business by listening to customers and mapping current processes.

M. Lind
Skanor Group Ltd, London, UK

K. Barner
Buyers Meeting Point, Shrewsbury, MA, USA

© The Author(s) 2018
M. Lind, K. Barner, *Finance Unleashed*, DOI 10.1007/978-3-319-66370-8_18

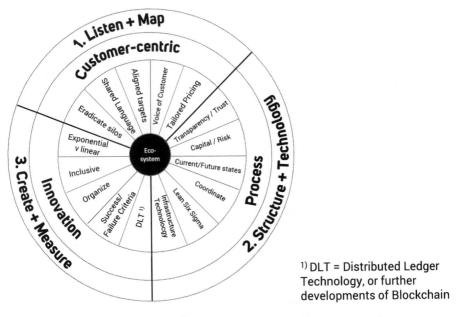

¹⁾ DLT = Distributed Ledger Technology, or further developments of Blockchain

Fig. 18.1 The practical model taking the CFO from here to there. Three steps to unleash finance

Voice of the Customer (VOC)

Understand what the customer needs and wants. Dig into the financial aspects you can add to your offering and engage with customers as well as your ecosystem. Use the Lean Six Sigma methods of the VOC we outlined in Chapter 17. Lead by example and actively engage in the process, for instance by conducting peer groups.

Financing the Customer

Consider financing customer purchases to increase the wallet of products and services they are able to buy from you. Lending your credit to customers to decrease their financing burden is nothing new. The trick is to do it so that you actually achieve increased revenues and larger profit margins, avoiding bad credit and managing your loan portfolio with reasonable default rates (and outsource credit risks where possible). This financing should not jeopardize your liquidity or lead regulators to regard you as a financial institution.

Introduce Advanced Pricing Capabilities to Drive Profit Gains

A 1 percent increase in profit margin has a huge impact on corporate performance.[1] Optimize pricing according to market segments or by better understanding customer demand patterns, openness, and willingness to pay. There is an abundance of data to analyze and you can obtain valuable information when interacting directly with customers. Mapping customer buying patterns will allow the company to individualize offerings, leading to higher spend and more targeted pricing.[2]

In Chapter 7 of *Confessions of the Pricing Man*,[3] Hermann Simon provides a good framework for the differentiation of prices of the same product to different customer segments and channels. For instance, Hermann advocates for price differentiation depending on the characteristics of the customer. If for instance, some customers are prepared to pay 800, others only 600, and your direct cost is 450, what price shall you take? 600 or 800? If you take 800 you earn more from fewer customers and if you take 600 you get more customers with lower margin. Herman suggests differentiating the type of customers and thereby increasing total profitability. Don't lose the 200 in extra margin on the customers prepared to pay more. (We propose you read Hermann's book.)

Payment Process Improvements

Reduce customer friction during the payment process and measure conversion rates and reasons for cancellations and lost business.

Reducing the transaction costs for payments typically includes reduced costs for card transactions. What other payment methods can you accept? Will you provide some loyalty program or financing schemes to incentivize the customer to use more cost effective payment methods?

Lowering Total Ecosystem Cost

Map capital costs and capital allocation in the total ecosystem and implement models to optimize allocation for lowest cost. Before implementing a costly and cumbersome system, solicit feedback from suppliers about what their capital actually costs them and where capital is being retained unnecessarily.

Finance the ecosystem of suppliers to lower total supply costs. The obvious solution here is supply chain financing techniques. If suppliers have a significantly higher financing cost, companies can also consider acquisitions, direct lending, or paying suppliers before or on delivery.

Multifaceted Risk Can Lead to Higher Prices for Customers

Map and manage financial risk (credit, foreign exchange, etc.) in the supply chain to lower total supply costs. This approach is more complex than providing cash financing and it often requires very close and continuous interaction with suppliers, which usually offers additional benefits as well.

Measure financial risk embedded in investment projects in the form of foreign exchange and commodity price fluctuations and manage their impact on prices paid and quality provided to customers.

Measure and manage country risk through detailed and up-to-date mitigation plans. Increasing country risk may serve as an early warning for an increased rate of company defaults in that country. Be proactive and support important customers to bridge any financial difficulties you can anticipate.

Finance Delivery

Measure how well finance is delivering in capital expenditure projects (cash available on time for instance). If financing a project unnecessarily delays production dates, it may negatively affect customer value.

Establishing Processes for Mapping Customer Centricity to Innovation

Financial Supply Chain Coordinator

Appoint a single point-of-contact for the financial supply chain, a coordinator responsible for building up your company's knowledge and efforts. Draw on experiences from how the physical supply chain was streamlined from the 1970s and onwards.

Current State Process Mapping

Follow how money is controlled and routed by creating a process map of the current financial supply chain. Use methods provided by Lean Six Sigma to understand current issues, for instance: poor flow, rework loops, delays, bottlenecks, and opportunities. Involve as much of the supply and demand chain as possible. When you have mapped your financial supply chain, you will gain a good picture of where it makes sense to start improving and inventing.

Future State Process Mapping

After you map the current financial supply chain, go further and document a desired future state. A model based on the financial supply chain might start with an understanding of where available cash is today, where it will be tomorrow, who controls it, and what costs and time delays you can affect.

Re-map Current and Future State Around Other Variables

For a comparison, re-map your financial supply chain, this time centered around flows of credit and funding (or trade finance, changing of ownerships of the goods, payments, etc.). Compare this with the current and future mapping you have done centered around cash flow. This way you will experience the best variable(s) to define the supply chain around for each purpose. For instance, if you want to allocate funds optimally, credit and funding would probably be best, as would using cash flow for decreasing fees and time elapsed.

Distributed Ledger Technology (DLT): Follow, Experiment and Stay Updated

Distributed Ledger Technology (DLT), such as Blockchain, is an opportunity for trade finance, payments, smart contracts, and elsewhere. Follow this area closely and be willing to experiment as opportunities appear to align with goals for the desired future state. DLT has the capability to turn the financial system and probably also your financial supply chain up-side-down.

Involve the Ecosystem

Participate in peer groups where you can meet your ecosystem to share experiences, ideas, and trends in the financial technology space. Broaden the group deliberately so it contains other industries, universities, researchers, vendors, banks, etc. Invite influencers and learn from cases in other areas. Involve the whole CFO's office.

Measure and Improve the Accuracy of Cash Forecasting

Consolidating the cash forecast requires experience and discipline, such as collecting reports from disparate systems, budgets, and reports. There are a plethora of systems supporting the financial supply chain: procure-to-pay, order-to-cash, treasury transactions, accounts payable, accounts receivable, etc.

There are two ways of forecasting cash flows: 'Bottom Up' and 'Top Down'. Bottom Up forecasting is a process through which operating units and group staff supply data to a centralized forecast while Top Down is based on central estimations on cash variations and flows. Many times, successful Bottom Up forecasting is developed under the pressure of severe cash constraints when cash generation hasn't been sufficient for some time or if the company is being taken private. Private companies usually have a far more accentuated cash focus than public companies. There are many successful examples where, by taking cash surplus out of an operation, cash discipline has been significantly enforced in the whole organization, not just in treasury. This is actually how many very successful entrepreneurs have built their companies, always forcing them to survive and grow on very scarce financial resources. Generally, the more discipline and strict rule setting in cash forecasting, the better accuracy. Note that cash forecasting is driven by data quality and not which IT system you use. During the financial crisis, many corporations realized that the most important enterprise risk was access to cash/liquidity, and their responses have developed best practice dramatically.[4]

Extend Cash Forecasting to the Whole Supply Chain

Cooperate with your ecosystem to map and optimize the cash flow fluctuations and improve forecasting.

How Unleashed CFOs Create and Measure Innovation

Creating competitive advantage by increasing the flow of ideas and fostering 'successful learnings' (or 'failures').

Make Innovation Inclusive

Aim to innovate inclusively instead of exclusively. Encourage everyone to participate by providing ideas, from the C-suite to individual contributors, and capture them in a structured way. Evaluate every idea and complete a feedback loop to allow for better results in the change management projects that will follow. The importance of continuously circling back is described by Jack Miles in Chapter 14.

Innovation Is a Discipline, Learn It

Train the finance department on design thinking[5] and invite inspiring transformational speakers to ignite ideas and provide broad perspectives. Using a methodology is critical: productive innovation is not creativity unleashed, it is a disciplined (albeit disruptive) process that organizations master the more often they do it.

Inside or Outside of Your Organization

Innovation may happen inside or outside of the company. There is always a risk that internal bureaucracy and policies will make it difficult for that innovation to thrive. In many cases, incubation is more likely to happen outside of the traditional organization in a 'free' environment with mentoring and specific support. Successful innovation will also need to be allowed to affect current parts of your company. Innovation must be strong enough to have the power to disrupt legacy business practices.

Involve the Whole Ecosystem

If you assume that innovation will emerge from within your own ranks, you may be restricting yourself too much. Proactively involve your whole ecosystem, including incubators and entrepreneurs in your industry and beyond. It is impossible to know who is best positioned to disrupt your current model, and the likelihood that it is a traditional competitor is lower than you might think. The biggest threat often comes from small entrepreneurial companies you have not heard of – yet.

Use Crowdsourcing

Crowdsourcing may innovate new solutions and reveal options not 'visible' to those already indoctrinated by existing internal practices in your industry. Crowdsourcing sites provide access to different perspectives and knowledge you don't have inside your own company (and perhaps not even in your ecosystem). Crowdsourcing can be a very valuable source of innovation, and a cost-effective one too. As Dwayne Spradlin, president and CEO of InnoCentive, asks "Is your world the laboratory, or the laboratory the world?"[6]

Create an Ecosystem Innovation Task Force

Invite a select number of suppliers, distributors, and customers to engage in special events focused on financial innovation. Set up a task force to work with them going forward to identify mutually beneficial opportunities, ensure the availability of sufficient resources, and establish a process for evaluating the opportunities that arise. Remember to circle back.

Define and Communicate Criteria for Success and Failure

Set up criteria to recognize successful innovation and to determine when and how to pull the plug on failed innovations. For inspiration, return to Murat Erden in Chapter 7.

Find Innovators

When you discover internal sources of innovation, find ways to retain and nurture the most able innovators, especially if they are Wealth Creators as defined by Adrian Atkinson in Chapter 9.

Find the Funds

Determine whether your company should raise money to invest in disrupting your industry. Liquidity is the key when agility – or the option to move quickly – emerges. Sufficient financing preserves the number of options that can be considered. Cash is (innovation) king![7]

Identify Areas with Exponential Potential

Figure out what areas of finance are candidates for exponential growth (performance/price doubling every 12–24 months)? Map them and aim to understand what implications, challenges, and opportunities they present.

One More Thing...

Since the core function of a bank is to finance the government, real estate, and households, it is only when banks have extra capacity that they also fund business and trade. If they lack that capacity (for instance, during a financial crisis), corporate banking is overshadowed by their higher priorities. The world's indebtedness has increased dramatically since the start of the Great Recession in 2008. Sooner or later, it is reasonable to expect that demand for credit will consume the full available capacity of the banks. This means that we should be prepared for the probability that corporate lending by banks will decline again, although hopefully not by as much as we saw in 2008–2010. Working through the financially difficult period from the end of 2008–2010 led to a dramatic corporate hoarding of cash. It also caused cash generation to be assigned a higher priority and regarded as a central metric.

A financial crisis is triggered by too much debt. Where are we in the global debt cycle? Do we currently have a strong or loose debt discipline? In the spring of 2017, we are experiencing the best of both worlds – high and increasing economic activity (and debt) and low interest rates that remain as though we are still in recession. Corporate lending from banks is currently easily available for large, well-rated companies. Can we assume that this situation is the new normal? Have we returned to a pre-crisis situation, where the availability of cash is likely to remain high over the long term? Will the cash always be this cheap? Is it safe to bet your company, and your supply chain, on those assumptions?

Large parts of the world continue to be in a period of considerable indebtedness according to the International Monetary Fund's World Fiscal Monitor from October 2016.[8] Why is the IMF concerned when so many new 'stability' regulations and policies have been implemented? The fact of the matter is that there is little, if any, empirical evidence that financial regulation leads to financial stability. Instead, financial crises emerge as the result of too much debt in the economy. At least that is what Carmen Reinhart and Kenneth Rogoff aimed to prove in their ironically titled book *This Time Is Different*.[9] (Too much) debt is an imbalance, and the more debt that is accrued, the more unbalanced the situation becomes. The volume of daily flows in the financial market created by the continuous reallocation of outstanding debt, collateral, and cash balances is mind-boggling. It is easy to realize that even small hiccups (such as the devastating but relatively minor Lehman Brothers collapse) can have such a huge and lasting effect. The likelihood of a financial crisis is equal to the level of debt. Why would we assume this time would be any different?

We believe the debt levels in the modern economy are something business leaders should adapt to and build their financial strategy upon. How will you ensure your company is properly funded through the next financial crisis, not to mention your supply and demand chain and your customers? Will you be able to rely on the banks, or even the capital markets, to sustain your supply chain during a crisis? What tools does the central bank community have time to build up again since they have used most of them in the aftermath of the latest crisis? So, who can the corporate sector rely upon for funding in the long term, if not itself? Surely this requires us to allocate capital more wisely.

It is not a stretch to predict that in the next crisis policy makers and regulators will (as in the most recent crisis) funnel the majority of available cash to the public sector.

From the 1980s until recently, government debt has been regarded as risk-free, and through regulation, banks are incentivized to invest in it. This 'free-ticket-to-ride' made many governments issue debt like there was no tomorrow and the banking system got used to regarding that debt as risk-free and its size a non-issue. Regulation had taken away the alarm systems, and the fact that regulators are paid by governments creates a risk of moral hazard.

The notion of 'risk-free' took a hit with the collapses of Greece, Italy, Ireland, Portugal, and Spain (the so called GIIPS countries) in 2009–2010. But it took until October of 2011 for the Bank of International Settlements (BIS) in Basel, the mother of core financial regulation, to admit the large mistake associated with assuming zero risk for sovereign debt.

In a paper published on October 26, 2011, BIS Deputy General Manager Hervé Hannoun described the problem as follows, "the regulatory treatment of sovereign risk could be seen as supporting 'financial repression' (i.e. policies that require private savings to be invested in government bonds and are likely to end up with a long-term misallocation of capital)".[10] The paper concludes: "Moving from denial to recognition of sovereign risk in bank regulation is one key element that will help to restore confidence and to foster fiscal discipline" and a "Need to put an end to the fiction of a uniform zero risk weight for sovereigns" thus admitting its fatal misconception.

What really happened in the 2008 crisis? Was it a bank crisis or was it instead a government debt crisis in disguise? How much did the banks receive as bailouts and how much have the banks increased their holdings of government debt? One example is when Spain had to borrow 100 billion euros in 2012 to recapitalize its banks after the Spanish economy experienced a burst of its multi-year housing bubble. How was that money used and how many hundreds of billions did the Spanish banks use to buy government bonds? In fact, who bailed whom out and what can we learn from this? How can we apply those learnings to prepare for the next crisis?[11,12]

The big risk becomes reality when the financial system's ability to create more debt reaches a limit. Since the global economic business model is built around constantly increasing debt, halting that process creates recessions. The faster the debt increases, the bigger the risk for a reversal.

Another factor is the exponential growth of performance over price relationships created by new technology. This factor will likely continue to limit inflation rates, which will in turn reduce the risk of increases in interest rates. However, interest rates are also used to support currencies that are deteriorating too quickly, which is an effect of highly indebted economies not finding enough investors to support their ballooning debt and forcing them to rely on funding from central banks. Japan is close to this situation. What risks does that imply for the currency rate of the Japanese Yen? Will future currency crises create interest rate hikes?

Perhaps most importantly, why is this relevant to corporate executives? The moral of the story is not to expect guaranteed help from an ailing financial system if you, or your supply chain, need cash during a crisis. It is therefore critical – not to mention strategic – to keep a focus on cash availability for you and your ecosystem. In a crisis, how else will you support your customers' buying power and your suppliers' staying power to support your business?

It is time to unleash finance.

Are you frightened by the lion?
Or,
Are you the lion?

Post Script: Thank you for taking the time and making the effort to read this book. We hope it has provided you with ideas and inspiration. And now, let's build further on the 'finance-unleashed' theme together. Please send us your ideas on how we can go forward from here. What more do you want to read about and explore? You reach us at advice@finance-unleashed.com.
Thank you!
Magnus and Kelly

Notes

1. Alex Hoff, "How to Optimize Pricing to Drive Margins and Customer Experience," *CFO Innovation*, May 22, 2017, https://www.cfoinnovation.com/story/13089/how-optimize-pricing-drive-margins-and-customer-experience.

2. Michael Reilly, "Google Now Tracks Your Credit Card Purchases and Connects Them to Its Online Profile of You," *MIT Technology Review*, May 25, 2017, https://www.technologyreview.com/s/607938/google-now-tracks-your-credit-card-purchases-and-connects-them-to-its-online-profile-of-you/?set=607959.

3. Hermann Simon, *Confessions of the Pricing Man* (New York: Springer, 2015).

4. Magnus Lind, "Cash Forecasting – Everything You Need to Know," *LinkedIn Publishing*, April 14, 2015, https://www.linkedin.com/pulse/cash-forecasting-everything-you-need-know-magnus-lind.

5. "Design Thinking," Accessed July 1, 2017, https://www.ideou.com/pages/design-thinking.

6. Big Think, "A Discussion About Crowdsourcing and Open Innovation with Dwayne Spradlin," *YouTube* Video, 10:49, https://www.youtube.com/watch?v=GrHcVikkH3k.

7. John Kinzer, "Why You Should Raise Money When You Don't Need To," *thinkgrowth.org*, May 19, 2017, https://thinkgrowth.org/why-you-should-raise-money-when-you-dont-need-to-365df0ad867d.

8. "Debt: Use It Wisely," *International Monetary Fund*, October 2016, https://www.imf.org/external/pubs/ft/fm/2016/02/pdf/fm1602.pdf.

9. Reinhart, Carmen M. and Kenneth S. Rogoff, *This Time Is Different: Eight Centuries of Financial Folly* (Princeton, New Jersey: Princeton University Press, 2009).

10. Hervé Hannoun, "Sovereign Risk in Bank Regulation and Supervision: Where Do We Stand?," *Deputy General Manager Bank for International Settlements*, October 26, 2011, http://www.bis.org/speeches/sp111026.pdf.

11. Daniel Woolls and Harold Heckled, "Spain's Banks, Government Co-dependent on Debt," *U.S. News and World Report*, June 25, 2012, http://www.usnews.com/news/world/articles/2012/06/25/spains-banks-government-co-dependent-on-debt.

12. Louise Armitstead, "Debt Crisis: Central Bank Action is Work of the Devil, says Germany's Jens Weidmann," *The Telegraph*, September 18, 2012, http://www.telegraph.co.uk/finance/financialcrisis/9551348/Debt-crisis-central-bank-action-is-work-of-the-devil-says-Germanys-Jens-Weidmann.html.

Appendix 1

How CFOs Prepare for Tomorrow

Faced with advances in financial technology and disruptive innovation, many CFOs are bracing themselves for even more change ahead—and understand that they must adapt to be effective. These are the results from a survey conducted by the authors in the first quarter of 2017 to understand how the CFO's office is changing with respect to the evolution of the financial supply chain.

n=92 respondents with the titles of CEO/Managing Director, CFO, Finance Director, Treasurer, Supply Chain Director, Sourcing Director, Procurement Director, and VP of Finance shared their views.

82 percent of the respondents indicated that their role was in a time of change (Fig. A1.1).

The additional detail in Fig. A1.2 illustrates the impact of change on how the respondents fulfill their role. We might expect that the professionals who chose to respond to this survey did so in part because they were predisposed to believe in the need to change their role to a greater degree than average peers. Since 41 percent need to rethink their priorities because of the changes to their role, and 7 percent are experiencing radically different expectations, we can anticipate the changes to be strategically significant. In addition, 34 percent said 'Yes' to the question.

Since the CFO's office usually contains multiple departments with different performance targets and practices, we asked what would be needed to increase the level of cross-functional cooperation. The top response (shown in Fig. A1.3) was to align targets between all departments in the CFO's office.

© The Author(s) 2018
M. Lind, K. Barner, *Finance Unleashed*, DOI 10.1007/978-3-319-66370-8

Is your role changing?

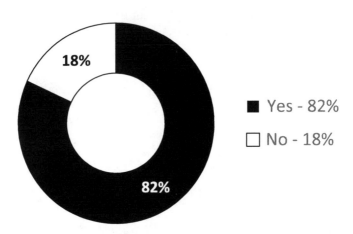

Fig. A1.1 82 percent of the respondents could relate to that their role in finance was changing to various degrees

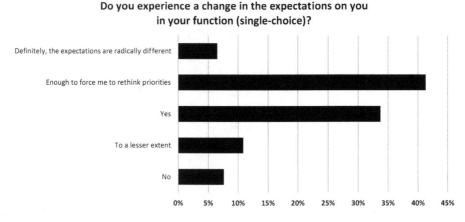

Fig. A1.2 Are you experiencing change in the expectations on you/your function? This was a single-choice question and a total of 41 percent + 7 percent experienced changes in priorities or radically different expectations

Typically, treasury has a working capital target that contradicts procurement's supplier cost target. Treasury strives to secure longer payment terms which can cause increases in the prices quoted by suppliers. If suppliers have higher capital costs than the buying organization, this approach increases the buyer's cost while reducing the working capital.

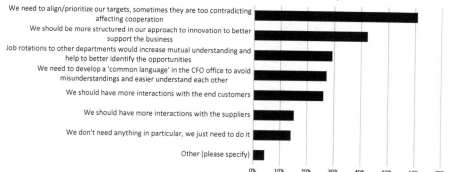

What would you need to increase cross-functional cooperation within finance (multi-choice)?

Fig. A1.3 What would you need to increase cross-functional cooperation within finance? This question was multiple choice and therefore the sum of the answers is greater than 100%

The second highest response was to increase the level of innovation as one activity to support business objectives. The third was to increase job rotation between departments, allowing individuals to experience other perspectives and challenges and also introduce new perspectives. Job rotation is expected to have positive effects on career progression and improve the retention of key staff.

The fourth need was to create a 'common language' to facilitate greater sharing and improved communication between the departments in the CFO's office. This may be more important than it appears at first look. Procurement and treasury usually have different perspectives, drivers, and objectives, confusing each other in the area of Supply Chain Finance for instance, a complex financial product that was historically initiated by treasury and maintained by procurement.

The need for a common language also applies when discussing supplier payment terms. For instance, treasury may be willing to accept a higher supplier price that implicitly means a bigger interest expense (covered up as a cost of supplies) than what the company would be able to obtain from their banks. This example is probably more common than we want to accept. Since procurement and treasury each use a different language to describe the situation, it may lead to misunderstandings and operational misalignment.

What are the ways forward for the CFO's office (shown in Fig. A1.4)? The respondents push for three top activities:

How will you improve finance? (multi-choice)

100%

57% Cross-Functional Cooperation

37% Full Supply Chain View

36% Participate in business modeling

Fig. A1.4 The three top choices to improve the finance function. This question was multiple choice and therefore the sum of the answers is greater than 100%

1. More cross-functional cooperation in the CFO's office (57 percent).
2. Taking a full supply chain view, especially of the financial supply chain (37 percent). We have drawn the conclusion that this action is so highly ranked because more and more executives realize the legacy approach of only focusing on the company's own balance sheet has to be replaced by a more holistic view.
3. Finance executives project themselves as being increasingly involved in business modeling or the core business of the company (36 percent). They also talk more openly about innovation as a tool for the CFO's office to provide value.

The full list of expectations for the future of the finance function also includes the trend towards automation and outsourcing to low-cost destinations. This is perhaps self-evident, since much of the work in the CFO's office involves massaging figures that are the results delivered by the business. In fact, a CFO's office produces limited value to the company's customers when it comes to the 'command and control' role. Standardization, automation, and simplification will likely lead companies to require fewer resources going forward than for the legacy CFO's office.

We find it interesting that almost one-third of the respondents expect to use alternative financing outside of the banks (Fig. A1.5). This is something we have experienced in our discussions with CFOs and treasurers in the past few years. There is a desire to circumvent the banking system for funding to avoid dependence on banks in a crisis, such as in 2009–10 when the banks' liquidity situation and risk aversion reduced lending to the corporate sector. Another reason to circumvent the banks is the actual credit risk they may represent, individually and as a sector. Corporations with large cash holdings

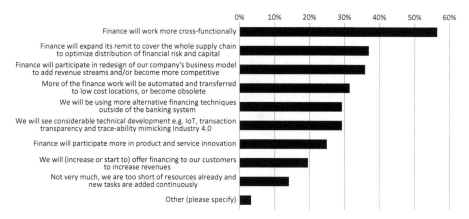

How do you expect your finance organization to develop over time (multi-choice)?

Fig. A1.5 How do you expect your finance organization to develop over time? This question was multiple choice and therefore the sum of the answers is greater than 100%

to invest often earmark one portion for non-bank risk investments such as corporate bonds and bills and money funds.

The introduction of Industry 4.0 also puts pressure on the CFO's office to make the financial supply chain far more efficient and lean. The dynamic, transparent, connected physical supply chain of Industry 4.0 can't rely on a fragmented, disconnected, non-standard financial chain.

Conclusions

1. Working cross-functionally in the CFO's office (and with outside stakeholders) requires the elimination of silos between its different departments. One of the best ways to break a silo is to build alignment towards one overarching objective, such as creating and increasing sustained customer value.
2. Silos are broken following the alignment of short-term targets and objectives allowing for the development of a shared 'language'. This creates the opportunity for the entire CFO's office to take a process flow perspective of the financial supply chain, using the same or similar techniques that have been successfully developed for the physical supply chain.

3. With shared objectives, a common language, and reliable tools, the CFO's office can be redeveloped to support the business migration to Industry 4.0. In addition, non-value-added activities can be eradicated, streamlining and optimizing the core operation.
4. This forms the basis for the CFO to participate in and implement financial innovation, providing value added activities to the customers of his or her company.

Appendix 2

How Treasury Supports the Business

The authors reached out to a large community of treasurers to explore the connections between their work and the success of the business as a whole. We conducted this survey in the summer of 2016. The respondents were mostly from the UK and Europe (Fig. A2.1), n=56. All respondents were senior treasury professionals in large multinational corporations.

The respondents listed 'supporting the business' as treasury's third most important task, and yet the same objective placed 11th on treasury's list of priorities (Fig. A2.2). What is the cause of this misalignment between their tasks and priorities? Are treasurers so focused on day-to-day operations that they are unable to take a longer-term view? Do treasurers have the time and energy to determine what it really means to support the business?

95 percent of the respondents regarded supporting the business as having at least a 'reasonably high priority' (Fig. A2.3). 66 percent regarded it as their highest or a very high priority. We can make a reasonable assumption that the professionals who chose to respond to this survey were predisposed towards a belief that treasury must support the business and, as a result, the priority assigned to this need would be lower in the treasury profession as a whole.

Finance and treasury are changing fast in response to new technology, increased focus on disruption and innovation, and redefined incumbent business models. Finance (including treasury) is seen as a possible competitive differentiator able to transform the company. Finance and treasury are expected to increase automation and cut costs, thereby providing better data analytics – an immediate and tangible benefit to the business.

© The Author(s) 2018
M. Lind, K. Barner, *Finance Unleashed*, DOI 10.1007/978-3-319-66370-8

Respondents' Location

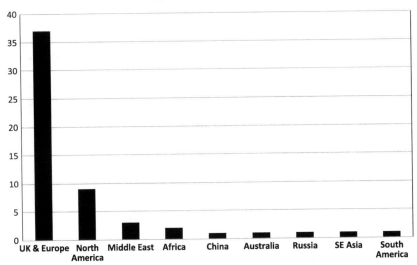

More than a third of the respondents were located in Europe or the UK

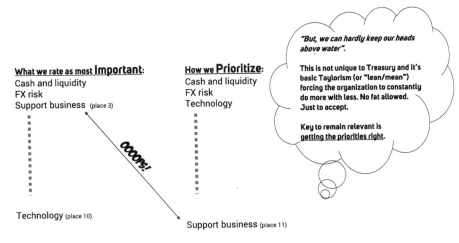

Fig. A2.2 Supporting the business is regarded as a very important task by the treasury, but it has a very low priority level (June 2016)

Almost all of the survey respondents (91 percent) have aspirations of taking on a more strategic role. We might expect that the professionals who chose to respond to this survey did so in part because they were predisposed to believe in the need to take on a business supporting function was greater than average desire of their peers (Fig. A2.4).

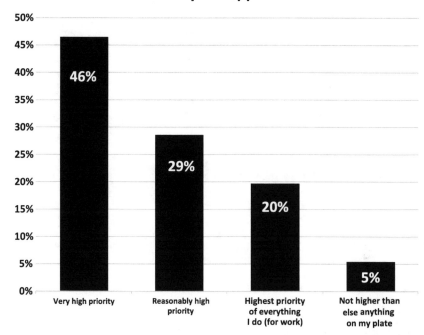

Fig. A2.3   How 'support the business' ranked in priority among treasurers

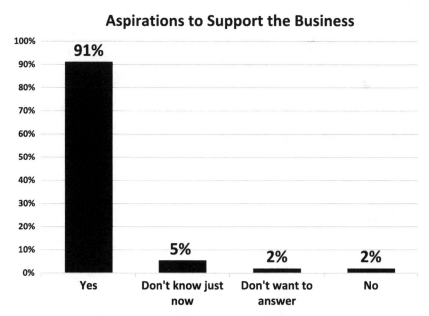

Fig. A2.4   The treasury's aspiration to support the business is high (91%)

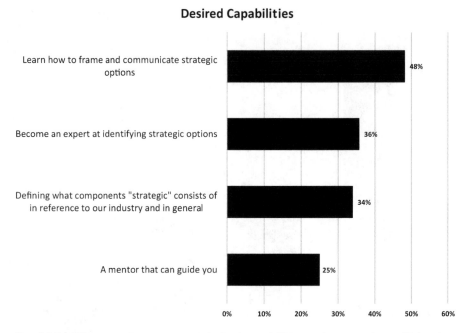

Desired Capabilities

Fig. A2.5 What are the treasurers' desired capabilities to learn and to self-develop into a business leadership role?

The rate of responses from our network of treasurers (1.7 percent of 3,336) could perhaps be interpreted as evidence that the forces of change are coming from outside of treasury instead of from within.

Figure A2.5 lists the desired capabilities (fixed answer alternatives and multiple choice) in order of importance. Treasurers seem to have the desire to understand how to frame and communicate their strategic options. This will require a combination of education (specifically focused on innovation models) and business modeling. Historically, these skills have not been strong in the treasury, since it has often been distanced from the actual business of the company. This distance has been gradually shrinking over the past few years, but it seems reasonable to expect business-minded treasurers to benefit from job rotation and experience with strategic business thinking.

We asked the question: 'How do you 'Support the Business' today?' with ten fixed answer alternatives (Fig. A2.6) and the customer-centric options received the lowest scores.

A deep dive into the answers in Fig. A2.6 confirms treasury's focus on delivering and managing liquidity, enterprise-wide risk and financing policies, and payment solutions, etc. It also confirms the lack of clarity about what it actually means to support the business in a customer-centric way.

Current Business Support

Fig. A2.6 How do treasurers support the business as of today (multiple choice)? The customer-centric role was geared towards customer financing (41%)

The treasury can directly support the business by providing customer financing, ensuring stable cash flows by managing financial risks, and securing sufficient liquidity and smooth, safe payments.

If treasury steps into an advisory role, it can provide guidance for negotiating payment conditions with clients and suppliers, show how foreign exchange impacts the business, work with the business to define cash needs at different working capital and investment levels, and align cash forecasting with operational flows.

Treasury can provide the business trade finance lines with standard wording and optimal pricing, help support entry into new countries, provide M&A funding and advice, and integrate acquired companies swiftly.

We believe treasury will change similarly to the whole CFO's office, where non-value activities (from the customer's perspective) will be automated and streamlined. For treasury to remain strategically relevant, it will gradually take on an increasingly customer-centric view. One opportunity is to take on a central role in defining and coordinating work over the financial supply chain. If treasury becomes a process owner from their position in the center of the financial supply chain, it will control the key suppliers (banks and fintech) and the cash flow and liquidity of the corporation.

The top long-term concerns of most CEOs typically fall into the areas of customer service, customer retention, and customer acquisition. The combination of these provides the base for corporate growth and survival. These tasks are very hard for a CEO to delegate when compared with cost cutting programs, for instance. We base this conclusion on our own experience and also on the opinions and research of others.[1,2,3]

CEOs delegate cost reduction, financing, and risk management, preserving improvement of the customer experience as their own direct responsibility. The disruption of legacy (or incumbent) business models has strengthened as a priority, causing innovation and digitalization to climb on the CEO's agenda as well. The largest disruptions and rationalizations will likely happen in the financial supply chain since it is remarkably inefficient and archaic.

Finance and treasury are experts on data management and digital transactions, providing them with extensive opportunities to take an increasingly strategic role and to become more customer-centric when setting the strategies and targets driving day-to-day operations. It is crucial for finance and treasury professionals to understand what the CEO needs and to act in response to that understanding.

Automation will free up time, allowing finance and treasury to remain relevant. We note that many finance executives claim they need more resources before they can employ a broader business perspective in their function. This is not unique to finance, however. It is instead a form of 'lean/mean' management that forces the organization to do more with less.

Conclusions

Supporting the business is a high priority objective for treasury; however, it ranks low when treasury is asked to prioritize their tasks. There are several ways we can interpret this finding:

1. The tactical and operational work of the treasury is so overwhelming that there is no time available for more strategic work.
2. What 'supporting the business' actually means is unclear, and treasury cannot translate it into well-defined priorities.
3. Treasury's business targets are not aligned with the overall business targets, creating ambiguity and friction.
4. IT solutions and management models are not configured to provide metrics to measure the level of support treasury provide the business, depriving them of a critical source of feedback.

Treasury is far from aligned with developing solutions for customers (as seen in Fig. A2.6), which is the essence of supporting the business. The current silo structure may simply be too rigid to support broad objectives. If all finance functions are siloed, the risk of conflicting targets increases, and treasury cannot change that paradigm alone.

Metrics for treasury often consist of detailed KPIs such as working capital, net interest costs, and foreign exchange exposures and gains/losses. How is treasury measured for their contributions towards customer success, retention, and acquisition? Are treasury's performance metrics pushing them to be tactical/operational even while the leadership team asks for more?

Notes

1. Jeff Thomson, "The Evolving Role of Finance from Spreadsheets to Strategy," *Forbes*, January 20, 2015, https://www.forbes.com/sites/jeffthomson/2015/01/20/the-evolving-role-of-finance-from-spreadsheets-to-strategy/#2427abf774ef.
2. "Four Faces of the CFO," *Deloitte*, Accessed July 2, 2017, https://www2.deloitte.com/us/en/pages/finance/articles/gx-cfo-role-responsibilities-organization-steward-operator-catalyst-strategist.html.
3. "New Skills Needed as Finance Role Expands," *Coupa Blog*, February 29, 2016, http://www.coupa.com/blog/new-skills-needed-as-finance-role-expands.

Bibliography

Christensen, Clayton M. 1997. *The Innovator's Dilemma: When New Technologies Cause Great Firms to Fail*. Boston: Harvard Business Review Press.

Christensen, Clayton M., Taddy Hall, Karen Dillon, and David S. Duncan. 2016. *Competing Against Luck: The Story of Innovation and Customer Choice*. New York: Harper Business.

Cialdini, Robert. 2016. *Pre-suasion: A Revolutionary Way to Influence and Persuade*. New York: Simon & Shuster.

Diamandis, Peter, and Steven Kotler. 2012. *Abundance: The Future Is Better Than You Think*. New York: Free Press.

Foster, Richard, and Sarah Kaplan. 2001. *Creative Destruction: Why Companies That Are Built to Last Underperform the Market – And How to Successfully Transform Them*. New York: Random House.

George, Michael L., John Maxey, David Rowlands, and Mark Price. 2005. *The Lean Six Sigma Pocket Toolbook: A Quick Reference Guide to 100 Tools for Improving Quality and Speed*. New York: McGraw Hill.

Greenspan, Alan. 2007. *The Age of Turbulence: Adventures in a New World*. New York: Penguin Group.

Griffin, G. Edward. 2010. *The Creature from Jekyll Island: A Second Look at the Federal Reserve*. New York: American Media.

Grove, Andrew S. 1995. *High Output Management*. New York: Vintage Books.

Harari, Yuval Noah. 2017. *Homo Deus – A Brief History of Tomorrow*. New York: Harper.

Ismail, Salim, Michael S. Malone, and Yuri van Geest. 2014. *Exponential Organizations: Why New Organizations Are Ten Times Better, Faster, and Cheaper Than Yours (and What to Do About It)*. New York: Diversion Books.

Kim, W. Chan, and Renée Mauborgne. 2015. *Blue Ocean Strategy, Expanded Edition: How to Create Uncontested Market Space and Make the Competition Irrelevant*. Boston: Harvard Business School Publishing.

© The Author(s) 2018
M. Lind, K. Barner, *Finance Unleashed*, DOI 10.1007/978-3-319-66370-8

King, Brett. 2014. *Breaking Banks: The Innovators, Rogues, and Strategists Rebooting Banking.* Singapore: Wiley.

Kurzweil, Ray. 1999. *The Age of Spiritual Machines: When Computers Exceed Human Intelligence.* New York: Penguin Group.

Kurzweil, Ray. 2005. *The Singularity Is Near: When Humans Transcend Biology.* New York: Penguin Group.

Linz, Carsten, Günter Müller-Stewens, and Alexander Zimmermann. 2017. *Radical Business Model Transformation: Gaining the Competitive Edge in a Disruptive World.* Philadelphia: Kogan Page Limited.

McGrath, Rita Gunter. 2013. *The End of Competitive Advantage: How to Keep Your Strategy Moving as Fast as Your Business.* Boston: Harvard Business School Publishing.

Nyden, Jeanette, Kate Vitasek, and David Frydlinger. 2013. *Getting to We: Negotiating Agreements for Highly Collaborative Relationships.* New York: Palgrave Macmillan.

Osterwalder, Alexander, and Yves Pigneur. 2010. *Business Model Generation: A Handbook for Visionaries, Game Changers, and Challengers.* New Jersey: John Wiley & Sons, Inc.

Ries, Eric. 2011. *The Lean Startup: How Today's Entrepreneurs Use Continuous Innovation to Create Radically Successful Businesses.* New York: Crown Business.

Ross, Alec. 2016. *The Industries of the Future.* New York: Simon & Schuster.

Schwab, Klaus. 2016. *The Fourth Industrial Revolution.* Switzerland: World Economic Forum.

Simon, Hermann. 2015. *Confessions of the Pricing Man.* New York: Springer.

Skinner, Chris. 2016. *ValueWeb: How Fintech Firms Are Using Bitcoin Blockchain and Mobile Technologies to Create the Internet of Value.* Singapore: Marshall Cavendish Business.

Templar, Simon, Erik Hofmann, and Charles Findlay. 2016. *Financing the End-to-End Supply Chain: A Reference Guide to Supply Chain Finance.* Philadelphia: Kogan Page Limited.

Thiel, Peter, and Blake Masters. 2014. *Zero to One: Notes on Startups, or How to Build the Future.* New York: Crown Business.

Vitasek, Kate, Karl Manrodt, and Jeanne Kling. 2012. *Vested: How P&G, McDonald's, and Microsoft Are Redefining Winning in Business Relationships.* New York: Palgrave Macmillan.

Vitasek, Kate, Mike Ledyard, and Karl Manrodt. 2013. *Vested Outsourcing, Second Edition: Five Rules That Will Transform Outsourcing.* New York: Palgrave Macmillan.

Index[1]

---

[1] Note: Page number followed by 'n' denotes note

© The Author(s) 2018
M. Lind, K. Barner, *Finance Unleashed*, DOI 10.1007/978-3-319-66370-8